DHARMA
THE WAY OF TRANSCENDENCE

BOOKS by
His Divine Grace A. C. Bhaktivedanta Swami Prabhupāda

Bhagavad-gītā As It Is
Śrīmad-Bhāgavatam (18 vols.; with disciples)
Śrī Caitanya-caritāmṛta (9 vols.)
The Nectar of Devotion
Kṛṣṇa, The Supreme Personality of Godhead
Teachings of Lord Caitanya
Śrī Īśopaniṣad
The Nectar of Instruction
Easy Journey to Other Planets
Kṛṣṇa Consciousness: The Topmost Yoga System
Perfect Questions, Perfect Answers
Teachings of Lord Kapila, the Son of Devahūti
Transcendental Teachings of Prahlāda Mahārāja
Dialectic Spiritualism—A Vedic View of Western Philosophy
Teachings of Queen Kuntī
Kṛṣṇa, the Reservoir of Pleasure
The Science of Self-Realization
The Path of Perfection
Search for Liberation
Life Comes from Life
The Perfection of Yoga
Beyond Birth and Death
On the Way to Kṛṣṇa
Rāja-vidyā: The King of Knowledge
Elevation to Kṛṣṇa Consciousness
Kṛṣṇa Consciousness: The Matchless Gift
The Nārada-bhakti-sūtra (with disciples)
The Mukunda-mālā-stotra (with disciples)
A Second Chance
The Journey of Self-Discovery
The Laws of Nature
Dharma: The Way of Transcendence
Renunciation Through Wisdom
Geetār-gan (Bengali)
Vairāgya-vidyā (Bengali)
Buddhi-yoga (Bengali)
Bhakti-ratna-boli (Bengali)
Back to Godhead magazine (founder)

A complete catalog is available upon request

The Bhaktivedanta
Book Trust
P.O. Box 324
Borehamwood, Herts.
WD6 1NB, U.K.

The Bhaktivedanta
Book Trust
P.O. Box 262
Botany, N.S.W.
2019, Australia

The Bhaktivedanta
Book Trust
3764 Watseka Ave.
Los Angeles
CA 90034, USA

DHARMA

THE WAY OF TRANSCENDENCE

His Divine Grace

A. C. BHAKTIVEDANTA SWAMI PRABHUPĀDA

Founder-Ācārya of the International Society for Krishna Consciousness

THE BHAKTIVEDANTA BOOK TRUST

Los Angeles • London • Stockholm • Bombay • Sydney • Hong Kong

ENDPAPERS: Lord Caitanya (right), and Lord Nityānanda appeared in West Bengal, India, five centuries ago. Lord Caitanya is Kṛṣṇa Himself, and Lord Nityānanda is Kṛṣṇa's primary expansion, Lord Balarāma. They appeared in order to wonderfully bless all souls suffering in the material world by spreading the congregational chanting of God's holy names, which is the prescribed dharma for this age, the Age of Kali.

Readers interested in the subject matter of this book are invited by the International Society for Krishna Consciousness to correspond with its secretary.

International Society for Krishna Consciousness
P.O. Box 34074
Los Angeles, California 90034
USA

Telephone: 1-800-927-4152
http://www.harekrishna.com
e-mail: letters@harekrishna.com

Bhaktivedanta Books Inc.
P.O. Box 262
Botany, NSW 1455
Australia

International Society for Krishna Consciousness
P.O. Box 324, Borehamwood
Herts., WD6 1NB, England

Telephone: 0181-905 1244
e-mail: bbl@com.bbt.se

Design: Arcita dāsa
Background photo: Māyapur sunrise by Arcita dāsa
Changing bodies: from a painting by Parīkṣit dāsa
Yogi: from a painting by Jadurāṇī-devī dāsī
Senses as horses: from a painting by Bharadvāja dāsa
Lord Kṛṣṇa with flute: from a painting by Dhruva Mahārāja dāsa

First Printing, 1998: 85,000
Second Printing, 2001: 57,500

Printed in Australia

ISBN 0-89213-326-0

CONTENTS

Introduction

Sanskrit words have become part of our everyday speech. For example, almost no one would need to crack a dictionary to understand such phrases as "media guru," "political pundit," or "bad karma."

Another Sanskrit word that has established itself in the mainstream of our language is "dharma." Fans of Beat-generation writer Jack Kerouac might recall his novel *Dharma Bums,* and in 1997 American television viewers saw the debut of a popular sitcom with a flighty new-age heroine named Dharma.

But what is dharma, really? If we consult the teachings of the sages of ancient India, we find there are two main meanings—nature and duty.

Let's first consider nature. Everything has its particular nature, a unique and essential quality that defines its existence. In this sense we can say that the dharma of sugar is its sweetness, or the dharma of water is its ability to quench our thirst with its pure taste.

Each of us has an essential nature, too, and if we live in harmony with our essential nature, or dharma, we feel deeply satisfied. But as human beings, what is our dharma? According to the timeless wisdom of the *Vedas,* our dharma is a characteristic not of our body but of our soul—the spark of divine consciousness within. Each of us has this spark within. It emanates from the Supreme Soul, Kṛṣṇa, who may be likened to a cosmic fire, the source of all the divine sparks that are our very selves.

And the dharma of each spark of divine consciousness is to dance in harmony around the central fire, Kṛṣṇa, the original supreme personality. We are all unique, individual, and personal manifestations of Kṛṣṇa, but our dharma is to recognize our source, to celebrate our eternal connection with Him through loving service. In short, our dharma, as eternally conscious selves, is to love and serve Kṛṣṇa, the Supreme Personality of Godhead.

In material consciousness we lose sight of our real nature. We forget our source and connection with Kṛṣṇa. And our original dharma of selfless service to Him transforms into the false dharma of competitive selfishness. Because we lose touch with our true dharma, we experience frustration and dissatisfaction.

Dharma: The Way of Transcendence guides us back to our true nature, our original position as loving servants of Kṛṣṇa.

Another meaning of dharma is "duty." In the latter part of the twentieth century we've experimented with the abandonment of a sense of duty and responsibility in favor of an ethic of self-gratification—"If it feels good, do it!" But now many of us are sensing that the experiment has failed. People are feeling that they've lost their moral bearings amidst a chaotic sea of hedonism. Duty is once again in favor.

But duty to whom, and for what? We can answer these questions only by understanding the other part of dharma—our essential characteristic. If our essential characteristic is to render loving service to Kṛṣṇa, then our primary duty is to focus our attention on awakening this loving service, or *bhakti,* in ourselves and helping others achieve the same goal.

Dharma can give us the insight and inspiritation we need. In this book, India's greatest spiritual ambassador to the world, His Divine Grace A. C. Bhaktivedanta Swami Prabhupāda, takes us to the very heart of dharma, exploring its meaning in his penetrating commentary on an ancient Sanskrit book called the *Śrīmad-Bhāgavatam,* renowned as the ripe fruit of the tree of Vedic knowledge. In the portion of the *Śrīmad-Bhāgavatam* Śrila Prabhupāda comments on here, the great sage Sūta Goswami concisely answers questions on dharma posed to him by an assembly of sages in the sacred Naimiṣāranya Forest (in present-day northern India).

There is nothing more important than understanding our dharma. This book thus stands as an enduring literary landmark for humanity as we move forward toward the new challenges and opportunities of the twenty-first century.

1
What Is Dharma?

. . . .

sa vai puṁsāṁ paro dharmo
yato bhaktir adhokṣaje
ahaituky apratihatā
yayātmā suprasīdati

The supreme occupation [dharma] for all humanity is that by which men can attain to loving devotional service unto the transcendent Lord. Such devotional service must be unmotivated and uninterrupted to completely satisfy the self.

Śrīmad-Bhāgavatam 1.2.6

In this statement, Śrī Sūta Gosvāmī answers the first question of the sages of Naimiṣāraṇya. The sages asked him to summarize the whole range of revealed scriptures and present the most essential part so that fallen people, or the people in general, might easily take it up. The *Vedas* prescribe two types of occupation for the human being. One is the *pravṛtti-mārga,* or the path of sense enjoyment, and the other is the *nivṛtti-mārga,* or the path of renunciation. The path of enjoyment is inferior, and the path of sacrifice for the supreme cause is superior.

The material existence of the living being is a diseased condition of actual life. Actual life is spiritual existence, or *brahma-bhūta* existence, where life is eternal, blissful, and full of knowledge. Material existence is temporary, illusory, and full of miseries. There is no happiness at all. There is just the futile attempt to get rid of the miseries, and temporary cessation of misery is falsely called happiness. Therefore, the path of progressive material enjoyment, which is temporary, miserable, and illusory, is inferior. But devotional service to the Supreme Lord, which leads one to eternal, blissful, and all-cognizant life, is called the superior quality of occupation. This is sometimes polluted when mixed with the inferior quality. For example, adoption of devotional service for material gain is certainly an obstruction to the progressive path of renunciation. Renunciation, or abnegation for ultimate good, is certainly a better occupation than enjoyment in the diseased condition of life. Such enjoyment only aggravates the symptoms of disease and increases its duration. Therefore devotional service to the Lord must be pure in quality, i.e., without the least desire for material enjoyment. One should therefore accept the superior quality of occupation in the form of the devotional service the Lord without any tinge of unnecessary desire, fruitive action, or philosophical speculation. This alone can lead one to perpetual solace in His service.

We have purposely denoted *dharma* as "occupation" because the root meaning of the word *dharma* is "that which sustains one's existence." A living being's sustenance of existence is to coordinate his activities with his eternal relationship with the Supreme Lord, Kṛṣṇa. Kṛṣṇa is the central pivot of living beings, and He is the all-attractive living entity, or eternal form, amongst all other living beings, or eternal forms. Each and every living being has his eternal form in the spiritual existence, and Kṛṣṇa is the eternal attraction for all of them. Kṛṣṇa is the complete whole, and everything else is His part and parcel. The relationship is one of the servant and the served. It is transcendental and is completely distinct from our experience in material existence. This relationship of servant and the served is the most congenial form of intimacy. One can realize it as devotional service progresses. Everyone should engage himself in that transcendental loving service of the Lord, even in the present conditioned state of material existence. That will gradually give one the clue to actual life and please him to complete satisfaction.

We are all hankering for complete self-satisfaction, or *ātma-suprasāda,* but first we must know what the real self is. The word *ātma,* or "self," refers to the body, the mind, and the soul. Actually, we are the spirit soul covered by two kinds of "garments." Just as a gentleman is covered by his coat and shirt, so I, the soul, am covered by a gross body consisting of the physical senses and a subtle body consisting of mind, intelligence, and false ego. A person covered by false ego identifies with his body. When asked who he is, he will answer, "I am an American" or "I am an Indian," etc. But these are bodily designations; they are not his real identity.

The Vedic literature teaches that one begins to understand his real identity when he thinks, *ahaṁ brahmāsmi:* "I am Brahman, or spirit soul." Therefore the *Vedānta-sūtra* says, *athāto brahma-jijñāsā:* "Now one should inquire about spirit." The human form of life is meant for advancing in knowledge of spirit, and this knowledge is the beginning of real happiness.

Everyone is hankering for happiness because by nature we are happy: *ānandamayo 'bhyāsāt.* As spirit souls we are naturally happy, blissful. But we are suffering because we have been covered by five gross material elements—earth, water, fire, air, and ether—and three subtle material elements—mind, intelligence, and false ego. Materialists, identifying themselves with these coverings, seek satisfaction through these gross and subtle elements of the body. In other words, they simply seek sense gratification, the happiness of the body. In the material world everyone is working hard only for this happiness. Some people try to be happy by gratifying the physical senses, and some try to be happy by gratifying the mind in such pursuits as art, poetry, and philosophy. But neither gross nor subtle sense gratification can give us real happiness, because real happiness belongs to the soul. And we actually see that although people are endeavoring throughout the whole world for bodily comforts, for sense gratification, they're not happy. They cannot be happy, because the basic principle of happiness is missing.

Suppose you have a nice coat. If you simply show the coat and iron the coat and keep it very carefully, you'll never be happy. Similarly, now you are trying to get happiness from gratifying the coat of the body, but that is not possible. Happiness comes only when you make the soul happy. Or, suppose you have a bird in a cage. If you simply polish the cage but do not give the bird any food, the bird will never be happy. Similarly, the material body is the cage of the soul, and if we simply care for the body, the soul will never become happy. So, the beginning of spiritual knowledge is to understand that the soul is encaged within the body and mind and that neither bodily comforts nor mental satisfaction will ever bring the soul real happiness.

Then how can the soul become happy? As stated in the present verse of the *Śrīmad-Bhāgavatam,* the soul can become happy only when living according to the supreme dharma. A common English translation for the word *dharma* is "religion," but, as mentioned above, a more accurate meaning is "that which sustains one's existence" or "one's essential characteristic." Everything has an essential characteristic. The essential characteristic of chili peppers, for instance, is to taste very hot. When we go to the market to purchase chili peppers, we test how hot they are. If they are not very hot, we reject them. So the dharma of chili peppers is to be very hot. Similarly, the dharma of sugar is to be sweet.

Then what is the dharma of the soul? When entrapped by the material nature, the soul adopts various artificial dharmas based on his false identification with the body. Someone born in a Hindu family will say, "I am a Hindu," someone born in a Muslim family will claim, "I am a Muslim," someone born in a Christian family will claim, "I am a Christian," and so on. But as I have already explained, one's real identity is the spirit soul—*ahaṁ brahmāsmi:* "I am Brahman, a spirit soul." When we come to that platform of spiritual understanding, our essential characteristic becomes clear. As explained here, *sa vai puṁsāṁ paro dharmo yato bhaktir adhokṣaje*. The supreme dharma of the soul is devotional service to God. That is our essential characteristic. Everyone is already a devotee—a devotee of his country, his society, his family, his wife, his children, his senses.

No one can say, "I do not serve anyone." You *must* serve, because that is your dharma. If a person has no one to serve, he keeps a cat or dog and serves it. So to render loving service to someone else is our essential characteristic. But we are missing the point. We are loving cats and dogs and so many other things, but we are neglecting to love God. Therefore, we are not getting real happiness. When we shall direct our love toward the proper object—Adhokṣaja, or Kṛṣṇa—we'll become happy.

When the word *dharma* is taken to mean "religion," we can understand from this verse of the *Śrīmad-Bhāgavatam* that rendering transcendental loving service to the Lord is the highest form of religion. The question asked by the sages at Naimiṣāraṇya was "What is the best form of religion, by which anyone can become elevated to spiritual emancipation?" Some people may say that the Hindu religion is best, others may recommend the Christian religion, others may say that the Muslim religion is very good, others may say that Buddhism is very good, and so on. But the *Śrīmad-Bhāgavatam* does not advocate the Hindu, Christian, Muslim, or Buddhist religion. It gives a general description of the best religion: "The best religious practice is that which enables you to become a devotee of Adhokṣaja."

"Adhokṣaja" is a Sanskrit name for the Supreme Personality of Godhead. The literal meaning of the name Adhokṣaja is "He who defeats, or 'pushes down' (*adha*), all efforts to understand Him by means of knowledge gained through sense perception (*akṣa-ja*)." This name of God—Adhokṣaja—is an answer to the mental speculators who research the question "What is God?" and write volumes of books. To them the name Adhokṣaja says, "You may go on speculating for many thousands of years, but you will never be able to understand God in that way."

Generally people say, "God is great." But they do not know *how* great He is. God's greatness is indicated perfectly by the name "Kṛṣṇa." If you want a perfect definition of the word "God," then it is *kṛṣṇa,* because the word *kṛṣṇa* means "all-attractive." Unless one is all-attractive, how can He be God, the greatest? If one is great, he must be attractive. For example,

John D. Rockefeller and Henry Ford were considered great men because they were very rich, and their great wealth made them attractive. So wealth is one feature of attraction. Therefore God must be the most wealthy person. Beauty is another attractive feature—so God must be the most beautiful person. Many people, when they see a picture of Kṛṣṇa, are convinced they have never seen such a beautiful person, although He's a little blackish. Similarly, Kṛṣṇa fully possesses the attractive opulences of strength, wisdom, fame, and renunciation. And because these six opulences of infinite wealth, beauty, strength, wisdom, fame, and renunciation make Him all-attractive, God is known by the name "Kṛṣṇa." With these transcendental opulences He can attract the richest person, the most beautiful person, the strongest person, the wisest person, the most famous person, and the most renounced person. Such infinite attractive features are impossible for us to understand through mental speculation based on sense perception, and so Kṛṣṇa is also known as Adhokṣaja, the name used in this verse of the *Śrīmad-Bhāgavatam*.

So, here the *Śrīmad-Bhāgavatam* gives a simple definition of the best religion: That religion is best by which you can develop your devotion and love for God. How nice this definition is! You may follow Christianity, Hinduism, Buddhism, Islam—it doesn't matter. But the test of your success is how far you have developed love of God. If you have developed your sense of love for God, you have actually followed religious principles. Religion does not mean that you go to a temple, mosque, or church and as a matter of formality observe some rituals, give some donation, and then come back home and do all kinds of nonsense. That is not religion. Suppose someone is said to be great. What is the proof of his greatness? He must have great riches, knowledge, influence, beauty, etc. Similarly, what is the proof that someone is a man of religious principles? The proof is that he has developed love of God. Then he is religious.

Now, someone may say, "Oh, yes, I love God." But what is the nature of that love? In our experience in this world we commonly see that a man will love a beautiful girl. But for how long? As long as she is beautiful. And a girl loves a boy—for how long? As long as his pocket is all right. This is not love: it is lust. "I love your skin, I love your money"—that is not love. Here the *Śrīmad-Bhāgavatam* states that love of God must be *ahaitukī,* free of selfish motivation. Not that we say, "My dear God, I love You because You supply me my daily bread." Whether in the church, temple, or mosque, people generally offer the same kind of prayer: "O God, give me my daily bread." In India people generally go to a temple and pray, "My dear Kṛṣṇa, I am in difficulty. Please get me out of it," or "I am in need of some money. Kindly give me a million dollars." This is not love of God.

Of course, this kind of religion is far better than atheism. As Lord Kṛṣṇa states in the *Bhagavad-gītā* (7.16): *catur-vidhā bhajante māṁ janāḥ sukṛtino 'rjuna.* Anyone who goes to God and asks for some benediction is a pious man. But he's not a devotee. He may be counted among pious men because he recognizes the supremacy of God, but he has not developed the highest principle of religion, love of God.

Lord Śrī Caitanya describes love of God in His *Śikṣāṣṭaka* (7):

yugāyitaṁ nimeṣeṇa cakṣuṣā prāvṛṣāyitam
śūnyāyitaṁ jagat sarvaṁ govinda-viraheṇa me

"O my dear Govinda! Because I cannot see You, every moment seems like twelve years to Me." Everyone has some experience of this feeling. If you love someone and you expect your beloved to come at any moment, you will feel as if every second were a full day. Then, because Lord Caitanya cannot see Kṛṣṇa, He says, *cakṣuṣā prāvṛṣāyitam:* "Tears are pouring from My eyes like torrents of rain," and *śūnyāyitaṁ jagat sarvam:* "I see the whole world as vacant." And all on account of separation from Govinda, or Kṛṣṇa: *govinda-viraheṇa me.* When you cannot tolerate separation from Govinda, that is pure, causeless love of God.

The next word used in the present verse of the *Śrīmad-Bhāgavatam* to describe pure love of God is *apratihatā,* which means "without being hampered for any reason." Sometimes people say, "I cannot love Kṛṣṇa because I am a very poor man," or "I cannot love Kṛṣṇa because I have no education—I cannot study Vedānta philosophy." No. To love Kṛṣṇa you don't require any material acquisition. You can begin developing your love of Kṛṣṇa simply by bringing some fruit or a flower to the temple and offering it to the Deity form of Kṛṣṇa. That is one of the six signs of love Rūpa Gosvāmī describes in his *Upadeśāmṛta* (4):

dadāti pratigṛhṇāti guhyam ākhyāti pṛcchati
bhuṅkte bhojayate caiva ṣaḍ-vidhaṁ prīti-lakṣaṇam

First, you must give something to your beloved and accept something from your beloved. If you simply go on accepting but you do not give anything, then there is no love. Then *guhyam ākhyāti pṛcchati:* You should not keep anything secret within your mind, and your beloved should not keep anything secret within his or her mind. And *bhuṅkte bhojayate caiva:* One should give the beloved eatables and accept eatables from him or her. When we cultivate these six kinds of loving exchanges with Kṛṣṇa, we develop pure love of God. And that love should be without any material motivation and without impediment.

If you can develop such love for God, you will feel *suprasīdati,* complete satisfaction. No more anxiety, no more dissatisfaction. You will feel that the whole world is full of pleasure (*viśvaṁ pūrṇa-sukhāyate*). So the best religion is that which teaches one how to become a lover of God, and the best welfare work is to distribute this knowledge. These are the purposes of the Kṛṣṇa consciousness movement. Kṛṣṇa consciousness is such a beautiful thing. It does not depend on any material acquisition, nor can it be checked by any impediment. In any part of the world, at home or away from home, you can chant the Hare Kṛṣṇa *mantra* in ecstasy and attain love of God very quickly.

2

Yes to Kṛṣṇa, No to Illusion

vāsudeve bhagavati
bhakti-yogaḥ prayojitaḥ
janayaty āśu vairāgyaṁ
jñānaṁ ca yad ahaitukam

By rendering devotional service unto the Personality of Godhead, Śrī Kṛṣṇa, one immediately acquires causeless knowledge and detachment from the world.

Śrīmad-Bhāgavatam 1.2.7

Those who consider devotional service to the Supreme Lord Śrī Kṛṣṇa to be something like material emotional affairs may argue that in the revealed scriptures, sacrifice, charity, austerity, knowledge, mystic powers, and similar other processes of transcendental realization are recommended. According to them, *bhakti,* or the devotional service of the Lord, is meant for those who cannot perform the high-grade activities. Generally it is said that the *bhakti* cult* is meant for the *śūdras, vaiśyas,* and the less intelligent woman class. But that is not the actual fact. The *bhakti* cult is the topmost of all transcendental activities, and therefore it is simultaneously sublime and easy. It is sublime for

*"A system of religious worship and ritual." (American Heritage Dictionary)

the pure devotees who are serious about getting in contact with the Supreme Lord, and it is easy for the neophytes who are just on the threshold of the house of *bhakti*. To achieve the contact of the Supreme Personality of Godhead Śrī Kṛṣṇa is a great science, and it is open for all living beings, including the *śūdras, vaiśyas,* women, and even those lower than the lowborn *śūdras,* so what to speak of the high-class men like the qualified *brāhmaṇas* and the great self-realized kings. The other high-grade activities, designated as sacrifice, charity, austerity, etc., are all corollary factors following the process of pure and scientific *bhakti*.

The principles of knowledge and detachment are two important factors on the path of transcendental realization. The whole spiritual process leads to perfect knowledge of everything material and spiritual, and the results of such perfect knowledge are that one becomes detached from material affection and becomes attached to spiritual activities. Becoming detached from material things does not mean becoming inert altogether, as men with a poor fund of knowledge think. *Naiṣkarmya* means not undertaking activities that will produce good or bad effects. Negation does not mean negation of the positive. Negation of the nonessentials does not meant negation of the essential. Similarly, detachment from material forms does not mean nullifying the positive form. The *bhakti* cult is meant for realization of the positive form. When the positive form is realized, the negative forms are automatically eliminated. Therefore, with the development of the *bhakti* cult, with the application of positive service to the positive form, one naturally becomes detached from inferior things, and one becomes attached to superior things. Similarly, the *bhakti* cult, being the supermost occupation of the living being, leads one out of material sense enjoyment. That is the sign of a pure devotee. He is not a fool, nor is he engaged in the inferior energies, nor does he have material values. This is not possible by dry reasoning. It actually happens by the grace of the Almighty. One who is a pure devotee has all other good qualities, namely knowledge, detachment, etc., but one who has only knowledge or detachment is not necessarily well acquainted with the principles of *bhakti*. *Bhakti* is the supermost occupation of the human being.

The knowledge that comes from practicing *bhakti* enables us to answer the question "What am I?" In the conditioned stage of life we pass our days not in knowledge but in ignorance, just like the animals. The animals have no self-knowledge. They are always absorbed in the bodily concept of life. The dog thinks, "I am a dog. I am this body." Of course, he does not know whether he is a dog or a cat. We have given him the name "dog." He simply knows, "I am this body, and I must meet the needs of this body somehow or other." That is his only business. The whole day and night he is simply working to meet the needs of his body. This is ignorance.

When we are no longer cats and dogs but are human beings, we can understand, "I am not this body; I am a spirit soul." Therefore the *Vedānta-sūtra* says, *athāto brahma-jijñāsā:* "Having achieved the human form of life, one should inquire into the Absolute Truth." The human body is achieved after transmigrating for many, many years through up to 8,000,000 lower forms of life. Therefore this life should not be spoiled by living like cats and dogs—simply eating, sleeping, defending, and engaging in sexual intercourse. These bodily demands are common to both animals and human beings. But what is the special facility of human life? The human being is eligible to understand what is the value of life, what are the problems of life, and how to make a solution to those problems. That is human life, not simply passing our days like cats and dogs, working very hard to satisfy our bodily demands.

Again and again the scriptures warn against this kind of degraded life. Lord Ṛṣabhadeva says (*Śrīmad-Bhāgavatam* 5.5.1), *nāyaṁ deho deha-bhājāṁ nṛ-loke kaṣṭān kāmān arhate viḍ-bhujāṁ ye:* "This human form of life is not meant for satisfying the senses with great difficulty, like the stool-eating hogs." Eating is necessary, of course, but a village hog eats the most abominable thing, stool, searching it out the whole day and night. And if human beings create a so-called civilization in which one simply has to work hard day and night to get food, then the lives of the human beings in that civilization are no better than the hog's life. That is not human life. Human life should be peaceful. One should be able to acquire food easily, eat nicely, and save time for cultivating Kṛṣṇa consciousness. That is human life. But if we create a civilization of cats, dogs, and hogs, then Kṛṣṇa will give us the chance to work day and night simply for eating, sleeping, mating, and defending. And that is the position now because people want it.

Actually, there is no scarcity of food. Kṛṣṇa is so kind that he is providing food for everyone (*eko bahūnāṁ yo vidadhāti kāmān*). He is feeding millions and trillions of living entities. Throughout the world there are billions of birds. Who is feeding them? Kṛṣṇa is feeding them. So the real problems in the world are not overpopulation or a scarcity of food. The problem is a scarcity of God consciousness. That is why people are suffering. That is not to say that the needs of the body should be neglected; they must be met. But we should not be busy simply for satisfying the needs of the body. We are spirit souls, and the spirit soul has its own needs. We must meet those needs. Then we will be happy.

These needs can be met when we follow the instructions of this verse and attain *jñāna* and *vairāgya,* knowledge and detachment. Detachment cannot be achieved without knowledge. Real knowledge means to understand, "I am not this body." As soon as we understand that we are not the body, we can also understand that sense gratification is not required. And that understanding is detachment, or *vairāgya.* But without *jñāna,* we think we must satisfy the senses. Absorbed in the bodily concept of life, which is *ajñāna,* or ignorance, we think our only business is to satisfy our senses.

The whole world is moving on the basis of sense gratification. When a young man and a young woman meet, the desire for sense gratification becomes very strong. As the *Śrīmad-Bhāgavatam* (5.5.8) says,

puṁsaḥ striyā mithunī-bhāvam etaṁ
tayor mitho hṛdaya-granthim āhuḥ

ato gṛha-kṣetra-sutāpta-vittair
janasya moho 'yam ahaṁ mameti

A man is attracted to a woman, and a woman is attracted to man, and as soon as they are united sexually, that mutual attraction becomes very strong. Then they are married and require a house or apartment (*gṛha*) and a job for earning money or some land for cultivating food (*kṣetra*). Then come children (*suta*), a widening circle of friends and relatives (*āpta*), and wealth (*vittaiḥ*). In this way the living entity becomes entangled in a network of illusion and thinks, "I am this body, and this family and property are mine."

Actually, nothing belongs to him. As soon as death comes, he has to change his body, and as soon as he changes his body, everything is finished. His property, his wife, his children, his country, his society—everything is lost. As Kṛṣṇa says in the *Bhagavad-gītā* (10.4), *mṛtyuḥ sarva-haraś cāham:* "As death, I take away everything." For His devotees Kṛṣṇa appears as Himself—as beautiful Śrī Kṛṣṇa playing a flute—but for the nondevotees Kṛṣṇa comes as death. Then they can see God. The atheists simply defy God, challenging "Where is your Kṛṣṇa? Where is God?" and in the end they also see Him, as death.

So the atheists and the theists both see Kṛṣṇa, but whereas the atheists see Him only at the end of their lives, as all-devouring death, the theists see Kṛṣṇa Himself in their hearts at every moment because they have developed love for Him (*premāñjana-cchurita-bhakti-vilocanena santaḥ sadaiva hṛdayeṣu vilokayanti*). The previous verse of the *Śrīmad-Bhāgavatam* (1.2.6) has described the culture of this love of God as the supreme dharma for human beings: *sa vai puṁsāṁ paro dharmo yato bhaktir adhokṣaje.* That culture is required. You may belong to any type of religion—Hindu, Muslim, Christian—but the test of how religious you are is how much you have developed love of Godhead. Without such development, your religious process is useless.

Sometimes people ask, "Have you seen God?" To see God is

not difficult. You simply have to qualify yourself to see Him by developing your love of Godhead. Then you can see God at every moment. This is the formula. And if you have not developed Kṛṣṇa consciousness to the degree that you can always see Him in your heart, then you can see God in the material world, as prescribed in the scriptures. For example, in the *Bhagavad-gītā* (7.8) Kṛṣṇa says, *raso 'ham apsu kaunteya:* "I am the taste of water." So, you can see Kṛṣṇa while drinking water if you remember, "The taste of this water is Kṛṣṇa." Is it very difficult? Not at all. Then Kṛṣṇa says, *prabhāsmi śaśi-sūryayoḥ:* "I am the light of the sun and the moon." If while drinking water you forget that Kṛṣṇa is the taste, you can see Him by remembering that He is the light of the sun and the moon. So when people ask, "Have you seen God?" we reply, "Yes, and you have also seen Him, because Kṛṣṇa says, 'I am the sunshine.'" Who has not seen the sunshine? So, you have to begin seeing God in this way—by remembering Him when you taste water, when you see the sunshine, and so on. Such remembrance of God is also seeing Him. Spiritual seeing is not done simply with the eyes. Because Kṛṣṇa is absolute, you can also see Him by chanting His name or by describing Him. *Śravaṇaṁ kīrtanaṁ viṣṇoḥ smaraṇaṁ pāda-sevanam.* When you hear of Kṛṣṇa, you are seeing Kṛṣṇa, when you chant about Kṛṣṇa, you are seeing Kṛṣṇa, when you are thinking of Kṛṣṇa, you are seeing Kṛṣṇa. This is the process for seeing God.

If you hear about Kṛṣṇa, if you chant about Kṛṣṇa, if you think about Kṛṣṇa, if you worship Kṛṣṇa, if you render some service to Kṛṣṇa, if you offer everything to Kṛṣṇa, you'll see Kṛṣṇa always, twenty-four hours a day. This is *bhakti-yoga.* My students in the Kṛṣṇa consciousness society are following these principles: They are cooking for Kṛṣṇa, dancing for Kṛṣṇa, singing for Kṛṣṇa, talking for Kṛṣṇa, going around the world for Kṛṣṇa—everything for Kṛṣṇa. Anyone can adopt these principles. Where is the difficulty? *Vāsudeve bhagavati bhakti-yogaḥ prayojitaḥ.* And if you practice Kṛṣṇa consciousness in this way, the result will be *janayaty āśu vairāgyaṁ jñānaṁ ca yad ahaitukam:* Very soon you will automatically attain knowledge and detachment.

The mystic *yogīs* are trying very hard to become detached from this material world by the processes of *yama* (proscriptions), *niyama* (prescribed duties), *āsana* (sitting postures), *prāṇāyāma* (breath control), *pratyāhāra* (withdrawal of the senses), *dhāraṇā* (concentration), *dhyāna* (meditation), and *samādhi* (trance). This is the eightfold mystic yogic system. And what is the goal? Detachment from the material world. Nowadays people take the goal of yoga to be health. But yoga is not actually meant for that purpose. Yoga is meant to detach us from matter and connect us with the Supreme. That is yoga.

There are various types of yoga, but the supreme yoga is described in the *Bhagavad-gītā* (6.47) by Kṛṣṇa as follows:

yoginām api sarveṣāṁ mad-gatenāntar-ātmanā
śraddhāvān bhajate yo māṁ sa me yuktatamo mataḥ

"And of all yogis, the one with great faith who always abides in Me, thinks of Me within himself, and renders transcendental loving service to Me—he is the most intimately united with Me in yoga and is the highest of all. That is My opinion." So the first-class yogi is he who is always thinking of Kṛṣṇa, and the easiest and simplest way to think of Kṛṣṇa is to chant Hare Kṛṣṇa, Hare Kṛṣṇa, Kṛṣṇa Kṛṣṇa, Hare Hare/ Hare Rāma, Hare Rāma, Rāma Rāma, Hare Hare. By this process your tongue, voice, and hearing process are all fixed on Kṛṣṇa. That is *samādhi,* absorption in thought of Kṛṣṇa.

This absorption in Kṛṣṇa, however, can come only if we are detached from the sense objects. As Kṛṣṇa says in the *Bhagavad-gītā* (2.44),

bhogaiśvarya-prasaktānāṁ tayāpahṛta-cetasām
vyavasāyātmikā buddhiḥ samādhau na vidhīyate

Those who are too much attached to material enjoyment and opulence cannot attain *samādhi,* absorption in Kṛṣṇa consciousness. They are thinking that material enjoyment and opulence will make them happy, and so they are called *apahṛta-cetasām,* bewildered. But if you practice *bhakti-yoga,* detachment will automatically come, and absorption in Kṛṣṇa consciousness will follow.

The whole Kṛṣṇa consciousness movement is based on the principles of knowledge and detachment. Now we are in ignorance, thinking, "I am this body, and I am attached to my bodily expansions—my wife, children, grandchildren, daughters-in-law, sons-in-law, and so on." In this way we gather our attachments around us. These attachments should not be rejected at once, but they should be dovetailed in Kṛṣṇa consciousness. This principle has been enunciated by Śrīla Rūpa Gosvāmī:

anāsaktasya viṣayān yathārham upayuñjataḥ
nirbandhaḥ kṛṣṇa-sambandhe yuktaṁ vairāgyam ucyate

A man and a woman should live together as householders in relationship with Kṛṣṇa, only for the purpose of discharging duties in His service. The husband, wife, and children should all be engaged in Kṛṣṇa conscious duties, and then all these bodily or material attachments will disappear. Every family can worship Vāsudeva, or Kṛṣṇa. You can install a small Deity or a picture of Kṛṣṇa in your house and perform worship. For instance, everyone has to cook food to eat. So, cook nice vegetarian foods for Kṛṣṇa, offer them to the Deity form or a picture of Kṛṣṇa, and then partake of the *prasādam,* or remnants. This is *bhakti-yoga.* It is not that the Deity should be installed only in the temple. Why not in your home? Although Kṛṣṇa is the *virāṭ-puruṣa,* with a form as big as the universe, He can also come within your room as a small Deity. *Aṇor aṇīyān mahato mahīyān:* God is smaller than the smallest and bigger than the biggest. That is His greatness.

So everyone can practice *bhakti-yoga* under the guidance of a bona fide spiritual master, one who knows the science of Kṛṣṇa. Don't lose this opportunity of human life. Practice *bhakti-yoga,* be Kṛṣṇa conscious, and make your life successful. Our mission is to teach this science. It is not a business—"Give me some money, and I will teach you." The knowledge is free. We are simply encouraging everyone, "Chant the Hare Kṛṣṇa *mantra.*" What is the difficulty? Simply chant Hare Kṛṣṇa and dance. Why go to some club to dance? The whole family can chant and dance at home. You will be happy. Then you will understand your constitutional position as servants of Kṛṣṇa.

This is the main mission of human life: to understand our position as servants of the Lord. This understanding naturally results in *vairāgya,* detachment. Two good examples are Sanātana Gosvāmī and Rūpa Gosvāmī, the foremost disciples of Śrī Caitanya Mahāprabhu. Before meeting Lord Caitanya they were the chief ministers of a king, Nawab Hussein Shah. They associated with highly aristocratic men. But after they met Śrī Caitanya Mahāprabhu they decided to retire from the king's service and join Lord Caitanya's Kṛṣṇa consciousness movement. About them it is said, *tyaktvā tūrṇam aśeṣa-maṇḍala-pati-śreṇīṁ sadā tuccha-vat:* Although they were big leaders of society, they quickly gave it all up as very insignificant. Then what did they do? *Bhūtvā dīna-gaṇeśakau karuṇayā kaupīna-kanthāśritau:* To benefit the whole human society, they became renounced mendicants and taught Kṛṣṇa consciousness.

Here the words *dīna-gaṇa* mean "the general mass of poor people." Rūpa Gosvāmī and Sanātana Gosvāmī saw that the people were very poor because they did not know the aim of life or the means for achieving it. One is actually poor who is poor in transcendental knowledge. Material poverty is no consideration. That may come or go, and one has to tolerate: *tāṁs titikṣasva bhārata.* And even if you have enough money, you will still be unhappy if you are poor in transcendental knowledge. Therefore transcendental knowledge is real wealth. That is why in India, the *brāhmaṇas*—those who were rich in knowledge because they understood the Supreme Brahman, Kṛṣṇa—were traditionally respected even by kings.

So we must become rich in knowledge and detachment. For so long we have been entangled in the materialistic way of life because of attachment. We live our life in ignorance, and after death we get another life, another body. Then another chapter begins. In this way our life is going on. Therefore we must attain detachment from this materialistic way of life so that we can end this changing from one body to another.

Unfortunately, people are so ignorant that they do not take this process of transmigration very seriously. They think, "Let us go on as we are. We don't mind getting another body. Whatever happens, happens." That is not very intelligent. You *must* have knowledge. This knowledge is imparted at the very beginning of Kṛṣṇa's teachings in the *Bhagavad-gītā* (2.11): *aśocyān anvaśocas tvaṁ prajñā-vādāṁś ca bhāṣase.* "Arjuna, you are talking like a big *paṇḍita,* but all your talk concerns this body, which no one should be overly concerned about." *Gatāsūn agatāsūṁś ca nānuśocanti paṇḍitāḥ:* "Real *paṇḍitas* are not very much concerned with this body, but fools and rascals are simply involved with bodily problems." This is *jñāna,* knowledge.

One can achieve this *jñāna* very easily. How? Kṛṣṇa explains in the *Bhagavad-gītā* (10.10):

teṣāṁ satata-yuktānāṁ bhajatāṁ prīti-pūrvakam
dadāmi buddhi-yogaṁ taṁ yena mām upayānti te

If you engage in the devotional service of the Supreme Personality of Godhead—Kṛṣṇa, or Vāsudeva—then Kṛṣṇa, who is within your heart, will impart knowledge to you. But that service must be rendered with love and faith, as we are teaching in the Kṛṣṇa consciousness movement. Since He is situated in your heart, Kṛṣṇa knows what you are. You cannot cheat Him. When He understands that you are serious about knowing Him, He supplies the knowledge by which you can go to Him. That knowledge is the process of *bhakti-yoga,* as Kṛṣṇa clearly says in the Eighteenth Chapter of the *Bhagavad-gītā* (18.55):

bhaktyā mām abhijānāti yāvān yaś cāsmi tattvataḥ
tato māṁ tattvato jñātvā viśate tad-anantaram

"One can understand Me as I am, as the Supreme Personality of Godhead, only by devotional service. And when one is in full consciousness of Me by such devotion, he can enter into the kingdom of God."

So, you do not need to make any separate endeavor to acquire knowledge. As stated in the present verse of *Śrīmad-Bhāgavatam, janayaty āśu vairāgyaṁ jñānaṁ ca yad ahaitukam:* "By serving Vāsudeva, one acquires causes knowledge and detachment." Thus a sincere devotee is perfect in knowledge because he is enlightened from within by the Supreme Personality of Godhead. As stated in the beginning of *Śrīmad-Bhāgavatam* (1.1.1), *tene brahma hṛdā ādi-kavaye:* "From within the heart, Kṛṣṇa gave Lord Brahmā the intelligence to create the universe." Similarly, He will also give you intelligence if you become His sincere servant.

As soon as you acquire this knowledge, you will naturally be reluctant to pursue material sense enjoyment. In the material world everyone is working in ignorance, trying to increase his own sense enjoyment, but in the spiritual world everyone is working in knowledge, trying to increase the sense enjoyment of the Supreme Personality of Godhead. In two lines the *Caitanya-caritāmṛta* (*Ādi-līlā* 4.165) very nicely explains the difference between material and spiritual motivation:

ātmendriya-prīti-vāñchā—tāre bali 'kāma'
kṛṣṇendriya-prīti-icchā dhare 'prema' nāma

"Wanting to satisfy the desires of one's own senses is called *kāma,* lust, and wanting to satisfy Kṛṣṇa's senses is called *prema,* pure loving devotion."

We see the contrast between *kāma* and *prema* in the behavior of Arjuna. At first he wanted to satisfy his own senses: "My dear Kṛṣṇa, I cannot possibly kill my cousin-brothers, my grandfather, or my teacher Droṇācārya." But after Kṛṣṇa had imparted the instructions of the *Bhagavad-gītā* to Arjuna and then asked him, "Now what is your decision?" Arjuna replied,

naṣṭo mohaḥ smṛtir labdhā tvat-prasādān mayācyuta
sthito 'smi gata-sandehaḥ kariṣye vacanaṁ tava

"My dear Kṛṣṇa, by Your grace all my is now gone and I have regained my original Kṛṣṇa consciousness." And what is his conclusion? "My duty is to satisfy You, not my senses." In this way Arjuna again came to his position as Kṛṣṇa's devotee and fought the Battle of Kurukṣetra.

Kṛṣṇa consciousness, pure love of God, is not something artificial. In the beginning you must follow the regulative principles of *bhakti-yoga*. Then after some time you will naturally get spontaneous love of God. As Lord Caitanya explains to Sanātana Gosvāmī in the *Caitanya-caritāmṛta* (*Madhya-līlā* 22.107),

> *nitya-siddha kṛṣṇa-prema 'sādhya' kabhu naya*
> *śravaṇādi-śuddha-citte karaye udaya*

"Pure love for Kṛṣṇa is eternally established in the hearts of all living entities. It is not something to be gained from another source. When the heart is purified by hearing and chanting about Kṛṣṇa, that love naturally awakens."

So, love for God is already there within each of us because we are part and parcel of Him, but that love is now covered by lust due to material association. When a mirror is covered by dust, you cannot see yourself reflected in it, but after you polish it you see your face clearly. Similarly, the process of *bhakti-yoga* polishes the mirror of your heart, and when it is nicely polished, you will see what you are and how you should work so that you will be happy. Everything will be revealed.

Therefore, our request is that you take this Kṛṣṇa consciousness movement very seriously and try to apply yourself in the service of Kṛṣṇa.

3

Seeing the Free Light And the Spirit

. . . . .

dharmaḥ svanuṣṭhitaḥ puṁsāṁ
viṣvaksena-kathāsu yaḥ
notpādayed yadi ratiṁ
śrama eva hi kevalam

The occupational activities a man performs according to his own position are only so much useless labor if they do not provoke attraction for the message of the Personality of Godhead.

Śrīmad-Bhāgavatam 1.2.8

There are different occupational activities in terms of man's different conceptions of life. To the gross materialist who cannot see anything beyond the gross material body, there is nothing beyond the senses. Therefore his occupational activities are limited to concentrated and extended selfishness. Concentrated selfishness centers on the personal body—this is generally seen amongst the lower animals. Extended selfishness is manifested in human society and centers on the family, society, community, nation, and world with a view to gross bodily comfort. Above these gross materialists are the mental speculators, who hover aloft in the mental spheres, and their occupational duties involve making poetry and philosophy or propagating some *ism* with the same aim of selfishness limited to the body and the mind. But above the body and mind is the dormant spirit soul, whose absence from the body makes the whole range of bodily and mental selfishness completely null and void. But less intelligent people have no information of the needs of the spirit soul.

Because foolish people have no information of the soul and how it is beyond the purview of the body and mind, they are not satisfied in the performance of their occupational duties. The question of the satisfaction of the self is raised herein. The self is beyond the gross body and subtle mind. He is the potent active principle of the body and mind. Without knowing the needs of the dormant soul, one cannot be happy simply with emolument of the body and mind. The body and the mind are but superfluous outer coverings of the spirit soul. The spirit soul's needs must be fulfilled. Simply by cleansing the cage of the bird, one does not satisfy the bird. One must actually know the needs of the bird himself.

The need of the spirit soul is that he wants to get out of the limited sphere of material bondage and fulfill his desire for complete freedom. He wants to get out of the covered walls of the greater universe. He wants to see the free light and the spirit. That complete freedom is achieved when he meets the complete spirit, the Personality of Godhead. There is a dormant affection for God within everyone; spiritual existence is manifested through the gross body and mind in the form of perverted affection for gross and subtle matter. Therefore we have to engage ourselves in occupational engagements that will evoke our divine consciousness. This is possible only by hearing and chanting the divine activities of the Supreme Lord, and any occupational activity that does not help one achieve attachment for hearing and chanting the transcendental message of Godhead is said herein to be simply a waste of time. This is because other occupational duties (whatever *ism* they may belong to) cannot give liberation to the soul. Even the activities of the salvationists are considered to be useless because of their failure to pick up the fountainhead of all liberties. The gross materialist can practically see that his material gain is limited only to time and space, either in this world or in the other. Even if he goes up to Svargaloka,* he will find no permanent abode for his hankering soul. The hankering soul must be satisfied by the perfect scientific process of perfect devotional service.

As we have already explained, rendering devotional service to God is the real dharma, or religion, for everyone in human society. People have manufactured so many religions according to their different circumstances and countries, but the essence is service to God. Suppose someone says, "I perfectly execute the ritualistic ceremonies described in my scripture and follow the tenets of my religion." That's very good. But what is the result? Whether you are following the Bible, the *Vedas,* or the Koran, the result must be that you are increasing your eagerness to hear about God. But if you believe that God has no form, that the ultimate truth is impersonal, what will you hear? Simply "God is formless," "God is formless," "God is formless"? How long can you go on like that? If God were formless, there would be no point in hearing about Him, because He would have no activities.

But God is not formless. He is a person, and therefore He has His form and activities. If God had no activities, why would He say in the *Bhagavad-gītā* (4.9),

janma karma ca me divyam evaṁ yo vetti tattvataḥ
tyaktvā dehaṁ punar janma naiti mām eti so 'rjuna

"One who knows the transcendental nature of My appearance and activities does not, upon leaving the body, take his birth again in this material world, but attains My eternal abode, O Arjuna"?

Here Kṛṣṇa says that He takes birth (*janma*), but this "birth" is simply like the rising of the sun. Actually, neither God nor the living entity takes birth. In the *Bhagavad-gītā* (2.20) Kṛṣṇa says, *na jāyate mriyate vā kadācit:* the living entities neither take birth nor die at any time. Then what is death and birth? For the living entities death and birth are simply changes of the body—the

*The heavenly planets within the material world.

gross body but not the subtle body of mind, intelligence, and ego.

Every night we "die." The gross body remains inactive on the bed, and the subtle body takes us away to dreamland. We may dream that we have gone to some friend and are talking with him, or that we are working in a different way than we do when awake. This daily experience proves that we have two kinds of bodies—the gross body of flesh and blood, and subtle body of mind, intelligence, and ego. We cannot see the subtle body, but it exists, as everyone knows. So, when death occurs we leave this "overcoat" of the gross body and are carried away by the subtle body into another "overcoat."

Because we cannot see the subtle body or the soul, we cannot see how the soul transmigrates from one gross body to another while the subtle body remains intact. When one is liberated, however, one is freed from even the subtle body and is promoted to the spiritual kingdom in a spiritual body. Therefore, while living in this gross body, we have to educate our subtle body in such a way that it becomes completely spiritualized.

That education is the process of Kṛṣṇa consciousness. If our mind is always thinking of Kṛṣṇa, and if we work intelligently for Kṛṣṇa, then our mind and intelligence will become spiritualized, and naturally our ego—our sense of "I am"—will also become spiritualized. At present we are thinking, "I am American," "I am Indian," "I am white," "I am black," and so on. This "I am" has to be changed. One has to simply think, "I am an eternal servant of Kṛṣṇa."

If you educate yourself in this way, transferring the activities of your subtle body from matter to spirit, then at the time of death you will give up your subtle body along with your gross body and go back home, back to Godhead, in your spiritual body. This process is taught in the Kṛṣṇa consciousness movement. The gross body we automatically give up at the time of death. Now we should learn how to give up the subtle body as well. For that one has to develop *prema,* love for God.

The first step in developing love for God is to acquire some *śraddhā*—faith or respect. For example, when someone comes to one of our Kṛṣṇa consciousness centers to hear about God, that is a sign of respect for the glorification of God. The person knows that he will hear about God, because our only business is to talk of God; in our centers we don't talk of politics or sociology or anything else but Kṛṣṇa. Discussion of those subordinate topics may come automatically, but our real business is to talk about God. And those who talk about God are called saintly persons, or transcendentalists.

There are two kinds of people in this world: transcendentalists and materialists. The transcendentalists, those who are interested in spiritual life, talk of God and self-realization, and the materialists talk of topics concerning the body—politics, sociology, welfare activities, and so on. A main source of these topics is the newspaper, which is filled up with news of this and that, advertisements, fashion pictures, and so on. The materialistic persons read the newspaper, but we read the *Śrīmad-Bhāgavatam.* That is the difference. We are reading and they are reading, but the subject matter is different. As Śukadeva Gosvāmī said to King Parīkṣit (*Śrīmad-Bhāgavatam* 2.1.2),

śrotavyādīni rājendra nṛṇāṁ santi sahasraśaḥ
apaśyatām ātma-tattvaṁ gṛheṣu gṛha-medhinām

"My dear king, there are many hundreds and thousands of topics for the materialistic person to hear." So many novels, books of so-called philosophy, newspapers, cinema magazines. All of this is of great interest to those who are *apaśyatām ātma-tattvam,* blind to self-realization, and *gṛheṣu gṛha-medhinām,* simply interested in maintaining the body, wife, children, house, and so on. Because they have no information of the soul, they are talking about the body, or sometimes about the mind. One philosopher theorizes something, and another philosopher theorizes something else, producing lots of literature that is all nonsensical because it is the result of mental speculation.

Often such speculation leads to atheism. Two classes of men always exist within this world: the atheists and theists, or the *asuras* and the *devas*. Therefore a class of atheists existed thousands of years ago in India. It is not that the atheist class developed recently. The number may have increased, but there have always been atheists. For example, long, long ago there lived an atheist named Cārvāka Muni. (He was known as a *muni,* a "thinker," because he was a mental speculator.) So, this Cārvāka Muni presented his atheistic philosophy as follows:

ṛṇaṁ kṛtvā ghṛtaṁ pibet yāvaj jīvet sukhaṁ jīvet
bhasmī-bhūtasya dehasya kutaḥ punar āgamano bhavet

Cārvāka's theory was that as long as you live you should eat as much ghee as possible. In India, ghee (clarified butter) is an essential ingredient in preparing many varieties of delicious foods. Since everyone wants to enjoy nice food, Cārvāka Muni advised that you eat as much ghee as possible. If you say, "I have no money. How shall I purchase ghee?" Cārvāka Muni, replies, "Then beg, borrow, or steal, but somehow or other get ghee and enjoy life." And if you further object that you will be held accountable for such sinful activities, Cārvāka Muni replies, "You will not be held accountable. As soon as your body is burned to ashes after death, everything is finished. So live joyfully, eat nicely, enjoy your senses, and finish your life." This is atheism, the philosophy of those who are *apaśyatām ātma-tattvam,* blind to the truth of the soul.

If you inform such people that the soul is transmigrating from one body to another among 8,400,000 species of life, they don't care. Even if you inform them that one who follows Cārvāka's philosophy is going to be a tree in his next life, they will reply frankly, "Oh, it doesn't matter; let me enjoy. If I become a tree, what is the harm? I shall forget this life." People have become so foolish that they have lost sight of their real self-interest. They are like children. Suppose you say to a child, "If you always play and do not go to school, you will not become educated, and then you will suffer in the future—you will have no position in society." The child may reply, "I do not care," but the certainty of suffering is there. Similarly, when you inform a modern person about the transmigration of the soul and explain that his sinful activities will cause him to become an animal, aquatic, or reptile in his next life, he will reply that he doesn't care or that he doesn't believe you. That is not very intelligent, because transmigration is a fact.

At every stage of life, one has a past, a present, and a future. A young man can remember his childhood, live in the present, and plan for his future as an old man. And why should there be no future for the old man? There *must* be a future, and that future is to get another body, whether it be the body of an animal, a tree, a demigod, or an associate of God. As Kṛṣṇa states in the *Bhagavad-gītā* (9.27),

> *yānti deva-vratā devān pitṝn yānti pitṛ-vratāḥ*
> *bhūtāni yānti bhūtejyā yānti mad-yājino 'pi mām*

"Those who worship the demigods will take birth among the demigods; those who worship the ancestors go to the ancestors; those who worship ghosts and spirits will take birth among such beings; and those who worship Me will live with Me."

So, you prepare yourself for your next body by how you act in this body. The ultimate goal is to get a body in the kingdom of God. That is the highest perfection (*saṁsiddhiṁ paramam*). Why? Kṛṣṇa explains, *mām upetya punar janma duḥkhālayam aśāśvatam nāpnuvanti.* "If someone comes to Me, then he does not get any more material bodies in the material world." What harm is there in staying in the material world? The harm is that every situation in this world is *duḥkhālayam aśāśvatam,* full of miseries and also temporary. Suppose you are an American. You may think, "In America there is enough money, vast land, and resources. I shall live perpetually as an American." No. You can live as an American for perhaps one hundred years, but you'll not be allowed to live as an American perpetually. Even Lord Brahmā, whose one day is millions of years long, is not allowed to remain perpetually in his position. The ant will not be allowed, the cat will not be allowed, the elephant will not be allowed, the man will not be allowed, the demigod will not be allowed to live forever. The great demon Hiraṇyakaśipu tried to live forever. He underwent severe penances to become immortal, but it was impossible. Of course, the lunatic scientists promise, "By scientific advancement we shall become immortal." But it is impossible.

Therefore, intelligent persons should try to achieve the ultimate transmigration, which is to go back home, back to Godhead. That should be the aim of life. Unfortunately, people do not know this. Therefore we are trying to render our humble service to human society by teaching, "You are attempting to become happy in so many ways, but instead of becoming happy you are becoming frustrated. So please take this Kṛṣṇa consciousness and you will actually become happy." Imparting this knowledge is our mission.

4

The True Goal of Dharma

dharmasya hy āpavargyasya
nārtho 'rthāyopakalpate
nārthasya dharmaikāntasya
kāmo lābhāya hi smṛtaḥ

All occupational engagements are certainly meant for ultimate liberation. They should never be performed for material gain. Furthermore, according to sages, one who is engaged in the ultimate occupational service should never use material gain to cultivate sense gratification.

Śrīmad-Bhāgavatam 1.2.9

We have already discussed that pure devotional service to the Lord is automatically followed by perfect knowledge and detachment from material existence. But there are those who consider that all kinds of different occupational engagements, including those of religion, are meant for material gain. The general tendency of any ordinary man in any part of the world is to gain some material profit in exchange for religious or any other occupational service. Even in the Vedic literatures, for all sorts of religious performances an allurement of material gain is offered, and most people are attracted by such allurements or blessings of religiosity. Why are such so-called men of religion allured by material gain? Because material gain can enable one to fulfill desires, which in turn satisfy sense gratification. This cycle of occupational engagements includes so-called religiosity followed by material gain and material gain followed by fulfillment of desires. Sense gratification is the general way for all sorts of fully occupied men. But in the statement of Sūta Gosvāmī, as per the verdict of the *Śrīmad-Bhāgavatam,* this way is nullified by the present verse, which describes the real purpose of religion.

Sūta Gosvāmī says, *dharmasya hy āpavargyasya:* the purpose of *dharma,* or a system of religion, is to take one along the path toward liberation from birth and death. The word *apavarga* is very significant: it means the negation of *pavarga,* the miseries of material existence. In Sanskrit linguistics, *pavarga* indicates the letters *pa, pha, ba, bha,* and *ma,* each of which stands for a different material misery. *Pa* indicates *pariśrama,* hard labor. In this material world, you have to work very hard for sense gratification. And *pha* indicates *phenilā,* foam. When you work very hard, foam sometimes comes from your mouth. We often see this among horses or other animals. *Ba* indicates *byarthatā,* frustration. In spite of working very hard, one feels frustrated. And *bha* indicates *bhaya,* fear. Although one works very hard, still one is fearful about what will happen. And finally, *ma* indicates *mṛtyu,* death. We work so hard, day and night, and still death comes. The scientific world is working so hard to defeat death, but the scientists themselves are dying. They cannot stop death. They can create some atom bomb to kill millions of people, but they cannot create something that will stop death. That is not possible. So, the word *pavarga*—indicating the letters *pa, pha, ba, bha,* and *ma*—represents five kinds of miseries in this material world.

Here Sūta Gosvāmī says, *dharmasya hy āpavargyasya:* by practicing religion one should nullify *pavarga*. No more hard labor, no more foaming at the mouth, no more frustration, no more fearfulness, no more death. In other words, our dharma must help us transcend the material world, because in the material world you have to work very, very hard and suffer the subsequent miseries. You cannot think, "Oh, I am such a great man that I'll not work." *Na hi suptasya siṁhasya praviśanti mukhe mṛgāḥ.* The lion is known as the king of the forest, but he still has to work. The lion cannot simply lie down and hope that some animal will come and say, "My dear lion, please open your mouth and let me enter." No. Even though he is the most powerful animal in the forest, he still must work very hard to acquire his food. Similarly, the President of the United States, though he is the most powerful man in the country, is working very hard in his post.

So, in this world no one can achieve anything without working hard. But we do not wish to work; therefore, at the end of the week we leave the city and enjoy some leisure so that we may forget all our hard labor throughout the week. Then on Monday we have to return to work. This is going on everywhere.

Being part and parcel of God, by nature every living entity wants to enjoy life without work. That is his tendency because that is what Kṛṣṇa is doing. Kṛṣṇa is always enjoying with Rādhārāṇī and the other *gopīs,* but He's not working. We don't hear from the *Śrīmad-Bhāgavatam* or any other Vedic literature that Kṛṣṇa has to go to His job in a great factory at nine o'clock and earn some money so that He can then enjoy with Rādhārāṇī. No. The Vedic statement is *na tasya kāryaṁ karaṇaṁ ca vidyate:* God has no duties to perform.

Then what is Kṛṣṇa doing? He is simply enjoying. Once a European gentleman went to Calcutta in search of a temple of God. He saw many temples of Kālī and some of Śiva, but only when he came to the temple of Rādhā-Kṛṣṇa did he say, "Here is God." Why? He remarked, "I saw that in the other temples Goddess Kālī and Lord Śiva are working, but here God is simply enjoying." This is confirmed in the *Vedānta-sūtra,* with the statement *ānandamayo 'bhyāsāt*—"The Lord is by nature full of transcendental happiness"—and also in the *Brahma-saṁhitā* (5.1), which states that Kṛṣṇa is *sac-cid-ānanda-vigrahaḥ,* possessed of an eternal form of knowledge and bliss.

So, just as God doesn't have to work but simply enjoys, we also want to enjoy without working. Yet even though we are Kṛṣṇa's parts and parcels and therefore also blissful by nature, because we have fallen under the influence of Kṛṣṇa's external, material energy, we have to work very hard just to live. We have to work so hard that foam sometimes comes from our mouth, yet still we are not assured of success. And we are always fearful because, after all, no matter how hard we work we must die. This is our position.

So, in the present verse of *Śrīmad-Bhāgavatam* (1.2.9) Sūta Gosvāmī says, *dharmasya hy āpavargyasya:* religion is meant to nullify these five kinds of material miseries—hard work, foaming at the mouth, frustration, fearfulness, and death. That is the purpose of dharma. Yet everywhere the Christians are going to church and praying, "O God, O Father, give us our daily bread." But God is supplying food to the cats and dogs and birds and bees and everyone. Why should He not give us our food? The proper prayer is "O God, please engage Me in Your service so I may be freed from these five tribulations." That is a proper prayer.

Of course, anyone who goes to church and prays to God for bread is a thousand times better than the rascal atheists who have no faith in God. They say, "Oh, what is God? I am God. By economic development I shall create so much bread. Why shall I go to church?" One who prays to God for bread is far better than such rascals because, after all, although he may not know what to pray for, at least he has faith in God. So he's pious. As Kṛṣṇa explains in the *Bhagavad-gītā* (7.16):

catur-vidhā bhajante māṁ janāḥ sukṛtino 'rjuna
ārto jijñāsur arthārthī jñānī ca bharatarṣabha

There are four kinds of pious people who come to God. The first is the distressed person. Any common man who is pious will pray to God when in distress: "My dear Lord, kindly rescue me from this difficulty." Then there are the poor people who go to a temple, mosque, or church to pray for some money. They are also pious. And the curious are also pious. They go to a church or temple thinking "What is God? Let us find out." Finally there are the learned scholars who are seriously searching after God and trying to understand Him. All these persons are pious.

On the other hand, one who denies the very existence of God, who tries to solve his problems solely by means of his own knowledge, is described by Kṛṣṇa as follows:

na māṁ duṣkṛtino mūḍhāḥ prapadyante narādhamāḥ
māyayāpahṛta-jñānā āsuraṁ bhāvam āśritāḥ

"Those miscreants who are grossly foolish, who are the lowest among mankind, whose knowledge is stolen by illusion, and who partake of the atheistic nature of demons do not surrender unto Me" (*Bhagavad-gītā* 7.15). One may ask, "There are so many big, big philosophers and scientists who do not recognize the existence of God. What about their knowledge?" Here Kṛṣṇa says, *māyayāpahṛta-jñānāḥ:* "Their knowledge has no value because the essence of all knowledge, knowledge of God, has been stolen away by illusion."

So, the *Bhagavad-gītā* says that only one who has faith in God is pious, and that among pious persons he who is serious about gaining knowledge of God is the best. Ultimately, religion, or dharma, is meant for those who are very serious about learning of God and getting out of this material, conditioned life. That is real dharma—not simply to go to a temple or church and ask God for some material benefit.

Preliminary dharma, however, does include such materially motivated religion as part of the four Vedic goals of life known as *dharma, artha, kāma,* and *mokṣa*. In the Vedic civilization, a person is recognized as a human being when he is interested in these four things: religiosity, economic development, sense gratification, and liberation. First of all one must practice some dharma, because without religious life a human being is simply an animal (*dharmeṇa hīnāḥ paśubhiḥ samānāḥ*). It doesn't matter whether one follows the Christian religion, the Hindu religion, the Muslim religion, or another religion, but one must follow *some* religion to qualify as a human being. Generally, people think, "If I become pious, my life will be nice. I'll get my subsistence." And actually that's a fact, because from dharma comes *artha,* money. And why do we want money? For sense gratification. And when we are baffled in our attempts at getting sense gratification, we want *mokṣa,* liberation from birth and death. Out of frustration we declare, *brahma satyaṁ jagan mithyā:* "This world is false, only Brahman is true."

But this is false renunciation. Real renunciation means to give up the process of sense gratification and apply yourself very seriously in the service of the Lord. In other words, renunciation means not to try to give up this world but to work in this world and give the fruits of our work to the service of Kṛṣṇa. Everyone is working in this material world to get some result. Whether you work piously or impiously, there must be some result. Nondevotees try to enjoy the result and become entangled, whereas devotees give the fruits to Kṛṣṇa and are liberated. As Kṛṣṇa explains in the *Bhagavad-gītā* (4.9):

yajñārthāt karmaṇo 'nyatra loko 'yaṁ karma-bandhanaḥ
tad-arthaṁ karma kaunteya mukta-saṅgaḥ samācara

"If you sacrifice the fruits of your work for Viṣṇu, or Kṛṣṇa, you will be liberated. Otherwise you will be bound up by the reactions of your work." Suppose you have performed pious work and are now a rich man's son. Wealth and good birth are some of the results of pious work, along with good education and beauty. And just the opposite results will accrue to those who perform impious activities: no riches, no beauty, no knowledge, no good family. But whether you perform pious or impious activities, you will be bound by the results and have to suffer birth and death in this material world.

So, generally people understand dharma in terms of pious and impious activities, but here the *Bhāgavatam* says, *dharmasya hy āpavargyasya nārtho 'rthāyopakalpate:* "Dharma should be executed not for material benefit but to nullify the miseries of material existence." Whether you are rich or poor, you have to undergo the tribulations of material existence. You may be a rich man, but still you cannot avoid working hard, you cannot avoid fearfulness, and you cannot avoid disease, old age, and death. And the same miseries are there for the poor man. So what is the benefit of practicing dharma in order to become rich? Real religion means to nullify the material miseries: *dharmasya hy āpavargyasya.*

Now, you may object, "But we require some money to maintain our existence." Yes, that's a fact. Therefore our principle is *yāvad artham:* By honest means you should earn as much money as you require to maintain your body and soul together. Don't work very hard simply to accumulate more and more money. That is the ass's life. In India a washerman will keep an ass to carry tons of laundry to the riverbank for washing. There he is let loose to eat a few morsels of grass. But while he's eating freely, waiting to return with the huge load of laundry, he does not think, "This grass is available everywhere, and I am free to go. Why am I working so hard for this washerman?" He has no sense to think like that, and therefore he's called an ass. Similarly, anyone who is working hard day and night simply to maintain himself and his family, without observing any principles of dharma, is simply a *mūḍha,* or ass. He has been collared by Māyā, or illusion.

We should earn as much as we need to keep body and soul together. Then we can use more of our time for getting free from the five miseries of materialistic life—hard labor, foaming at the mouth, frustration, fear, and death. That is dharma. And if by practicing dharma you get more money than you need, don't spend it for sense gratification but employ it in the service of Kṛṣṇa. In days gone by, rich men would often construct a church, temple, or mosque. That was the system throughout the whole world because people knew that if they had some extra money they should employ it in the service of God. But at present many churches are being transformed into factories because people have lost religion. And because they have lost religion, they are animals. And how you can have peace and prosperity in a society of animals?

So, here in the *Śrīmad-Bhāgavatam* Sūta Gosvāmī is explaining that to become peaceful and satisfied, one must practice first-class *dharma.* First he says:

sa vai puṁsāṁ paro dharmo yato bhaktir adhokṣaje
ahaituky apratihatā yayātmā suprasīdati

"If you want peace of mind, if you want full satisfaction, then you must practice that dharma, or religion, by which you will advance in unmotivated, uninterrupted devotional service to the Lord" (*Śrīmad-Bhāgavatam* 1.2.6).

Then he says,

vāsudeve bhagavati bhakti-yogaḥ prayojitaḥ
janayaty āśu vairāgyaṁ jñānaṁ ca yad ahaitukam

"If you devote yourself to the service of Vāsudeva (Kṛṣṇa), you will quickly get perfect knowledge and renunciation without any doubt" (*Śrīmad-Bhāgavatam* 1.2.7).

Next he warns,

dharmaḥ svanuṣṭhitaḥ puṁsāṁ viṣvaksena-kathāsu yaḥ
notpādayed yadi ratiṁ śrama eva hi kevalam

"If you do not develop your consciousness of God by executing your religious principles, then you are simply wasting your time and labor" (*Śrīmad-Bhāgavatam* 1.2.7).

And now in the present verse Sūta Gosvāmī says,

dharmasya hy āpavargyasya nārtho 'rthāyopakalpate
nārthasya dharmaikāntasya kāmo lābhāya hi smṛtaḥ

"One should not engage in any dharma only for material gain, nor should one use material gain for sense gratification." How one *should* use material gain is described in the next verse.

So, the *Śrīmad-Bhāgavatam* is meant for giving enlightenment to all people of the world. It is not the philosophy of a sectarian religion; it is meant for all human beings. People should take advantage of the instructions in the *Śrīmad-Bhāgavatam* and make their lives perfect. That is the mission of our Kṛṣṇa consciousness movement.

5

What the Senses Are Meant For

kāmasya nendriya-prītir
lābho jīveta yāvatā
jīvasya tattva-jijñāsā
nārtho yaś ceha karmabhiḥ

Life's desires should never be directed toward sense gratification. One should desire only a healthy life, or self-preservation, since a human being is meant for inquiry about the Absolute Truth. Nothing else should be the goal of one's works.

Śrīmad-Bhāgavatam 1.2.10

The completely bewildered material civilization is wrongly directed toward the fulfillment of desires in sense gratification. In such a civilization, in all spheres of life, the ultimate end is sense gratification. In politics, social service, altruism, philanthropy, and ultimately in religion or even in salvation, the very same tint of sense gratification is ever-increasingly predominant. In the political field the leaders of men fight with one another to fulfill their personal sense gratification. The voters adore the so-called leaders only when they promise sense gratification. As soon as the voters are dissatisfied in their own sense satisfaction, they dethrone the leaders. The leaders must always disappoint the voters by not satisfying their senses. The same is applicable in all other fields; no one is serious about the problems of life. Even those who are on the path of salvation desire to become one with the Absolute Truth and desire to commit spiritual suicide for sense gratification.

But here the *Bhāgavatam* says that one should not live for sense gratification. One should satisfy the senses only insomuch as required for self-preservation, and not for sense gratification. Because the body is made of senses, which also require a certain amount of satisfaction, there are regulative directions for satisfaction of such senses. But the senses are not meant for unrestricted enjoyment. For example, marriage, or the combination of a man with a woman, is necessary for progeny, but it is not meant for sense enjoyment. In the absence of voluntary restraint, there is propaganda for family planning, but foolish men do not know that family planning is automatically executed as soon as there is the search after the Absolute Truth. Seekers of the Absolute Truth are never allured by unnecessary engagements in sense gratification because the serious students seeking the Absolute Truth are always overwhelmed with the work of researching the Truth. In every sphere of life, therefore, the ultimate end must be seeking after the Absolute Truth, and that sort of engagement will make one happy because one will be less engaged in varieties of sense gratification.

The business of human beings is not simply to eat, sleep, have sex, and defend. That may be the business of the cats and dogs, but human life is meant for a higher purpose. Human civilization should be molded so that people will have the chance to think soberly about the truth of life—to inquire about God, this material nature, our relationship with God and with nature, and so on. That is called *tattva-jijñāsā,* inquiry into the Absolute Truth. It is everyone's duty to inquire into the Absolute Truth. There is no question of this being the duty of the Hindus but not the Muslims and the Christians. Truth is truth. That two plus two equals four is accepted by the Hindus, the Muslims, the Christians, and everyone else. Science is science. Therefore everyone should be inquisitive about the science of the Absolute Truth.

Where to inquire into the Absolute Truth? The *Bhāgavatam* (11.3.21) says, *tasmād gurum prapadyeta jijñāsuḥ śreya uttamam:* "Those who are inquisitive to know the Absolute Truth must approach a guru." As in the present verse of the *Bhāgavatam,* the word *jijñāsā,* "inquisitive," is also used in this verse from the Eleventh Canto. This word is used when someone in an inferior position inquires from a superior. For example, when a child inquires from his father, that is *jijñāsā.* An intelligent child always inquires, "Father, what is this? What is that?" and the father explains. In this way the child gets knowledge.

From whom should you inquire about the Absolute Truth? Kṛṣṇa answers in the *Bhagavad-gītā* (4.34): *upadekṣyanti te jñānaṁ jñāninas tattva-darśinaḥ.* Those who have actually seen the Absolute Truth (the *tattva-darśīs*) can give you knowledge of the Absolute Truth. According to the Vedic scriptures, a *tattva-darśī* should be very pure. Therefore, one should generally go to a qualified *brāhmaṇa* to inquire about the Absolute Truth. Lord Kṛṣṇa gives the qualities of a *brāhmaṇa* in the *Bhagavad-gītā* (18.42):

śamo damas tapaḥ śaucaṁ kṣāntir ārjavam eva ca
jñānaṁ vijñānam āstikyaṁ brahma-karma svabhāva-jam

"Peacefulness, self-control, austerity, purity, tolerance, honesty, knowledge, wisdom, and religiousness—these are the natural qualities by which the *brāhmaṇas* work."

So, in the Vedic system the first qualification of a guru is that he must be a *brāhmaṇa.* He need not have taken birth in a *brāhmaṇa* family, but he must possess the qualities of a *brāhmaṇa*. Still, even if he has the qualities of a *brāhmaṇa*, he cannot become a guru if he is not a Vaiṣṇava. That is the injunction of the *śāstra:*

ṣaṭ-karma-nipuṇo vipro mantra-tantra-viśāradaḥ
avaiṣṇavo gurur na syād vaiṣṇavaḥ śva-paco guruḥ

"Even if a *brāhmaṇa* is very learned in the Vedic scriptures and knows the six occupational duties of a *brāhmaṇa,** he cannot become a spiritual master unless he is a devotee of the Supreme Personality of Godhead. However, if one is born in a family of dog-eaters but is a pure devotee of the Lord, he can become a spiritual master."

So a guru has to be a Vaiṣṇava, a devotee of the Supreme Personality of Godhead. Otherwise, he cannot know Lord Kṛṣṇa in truth. As Kṛṣṇa says to Arjuna in the *Bhagavad-gītā* (4.3), *bhakto 'si me sakhā ceti rahasyaṁ hy etad uttamam:* "My dear Arjuna, it is because you are My devotee and friend that you can understand this secret science of Kṛṣṇa consciousness I am speaking to you." Therefore the guru must be a devotee of Kṛṣṇa, or in other words Kṛṣṇa's representative.

By serving the guru and inquiring from him, we can come to the point where Kṛṣṇa will enlighten us from within. Kṛṣṇa, the supreme guru, first imparted knowledge into the heart of Brahmā, the original person in the universe (*tene brahma hṛdā ādi-kavaye*). Kṛṣṇa is situated in everyone's heart as the Supersoul, and as you become purified He speaks to you from within. Actually, He is always speaking to us, but in our impure condition we cannot hear Him. In the *Bhagavad-gītā* (15.15) Kṛṣṇa confirms that He is the source of our knowledge: *sarvasya cāhaṁ hṛdi sanniviṣṭo mattaḥ smṛtir jñānam apohanaṁ ca.* "I am situated within the heart of everyone, and from Me come all remembrance, knowledge, and forgetfulness." So as Paramātmā, the Supersoul, Kṛṣṇa is always prepared to help every one of us, provided we serve Him and take His instruction. He says in the *Bhagavad-gītā* (10.10),

teṣāṁ satata-yuktānāṁ bhajatāṁ prīti-pūrvakam
dadāmi buddhi-yogaṁ taṁ yena mām upayānti te

"To those who are always engaged in serving Me with great love

---

*The six duties of a *brāhmaṇa* are (1) to become well versed in the Vedic literatures, (2) to teach this knowledge, (3) to expertly worship the Lord and the demigods, (4) to teach others how to worship, (5) to accept charity, and (6) to give charity.

and devotion, I give the understanding by which they can come to Me."

If we want to know the Absolute Truth, we have to follow the proper process, and that process is simply to engage oneself in the loving service of the Lord. That will enable us one day to directly perceive the Absolute Truth. With our present blunt material senses we cannot perceive the Absolute Truth, the Supreme Personality of Godhead. For example, with a blunt knife you cannot cut anything. You must sharpen it first; then it cuts very nicely. Similarly, to understand the Absolute Truth you must sharpen and purify your senses by engaging them in the service of the Lord. Now you cannot see God, or Kṛṣṇa. But if you purify your eyes and your other senses, you will be able to see God, to hear God, to talk with God—everything. That is possible by the process of *bhakti.*

The *Nārada-pañcarātra* defines *bhakti* as follows:

sarvopādhi-vinirmuktaṁ tat-paratvena nirmalam
hṛṣīkeṇa hṛṣīkeśa-sevanaṁ bhaktir ucyate

Now we are deluded by so many material designations (*upādhis*), and so we are misusing our senses. For instance, we may think, "This hand is my hand and I will use it for my purposes," or "Let me use this hand for my family, my community, or my nation." Actually the hand belongs to Kṛṣṇa and should therefore be used for His purposes, not for anything else. That is why one of Kṛṣṇa's names is Hṛṣīkeśa, the master of the senses. When we actually engage our senses in the service of Kṛṣṇa, we become free of material designations and our senses become purified. This is *bhakti,* or Kṛṣṇa consciousness.

Everyone should awaken to this consciousness, beginning with *tattva-jijñāsā,* inquiry into the Absolute Truth. The answers to your inquiries have been provided by Kṛṣṇa in so many books of knowledge—the *Śrīmad-Bhāgavatam,* the *Bhagavad-gītā,* and so on. We should take advantage of this treasure house of knowledge. But instead of utilizing this knowledge, people are reading bunches of useless newspapers. In the morning the newspaper is delivered, and after one hour it is thrown away. In this way people's attention is being diverted by so much nonsense literature, and no one is interested in inquiring about the Absolute Truth from the real treasure house of knowledge, the *Śrīmad-Bhāgavatam.* Therefore in the present verse the *Bhāgavatam* warns, *jīvasya tattva-jijñāsā nārtho yaś ceha karmibhiḥ:* "Your only business is to inquire about the Absolute Truth." And what that Absolute Truth is is explained in detail in the next verse.

6

Defining The Absolute Truth

vadanti tat tattva-vidas
tattvaṁ yaj jñānam advayam
brahmeti paramātmeti
bhagavān iti śabdyate

Learned transcendentalists who know the Absolute Truth call this nondual substance Brahman, Paramātmā or Bhagavān.

Śrīmad-Bhāgavatam 1.2.11

The Absolute Truth is both subject and object, and there is no qualitative difference there. Therefore, Brahman, Paramātmā, and Bhagavān are qualitatively one and the same. The same substance is realized as impersonal Brahman by the students of the *Upaniṣads,* as localized Paramātmā by the Hiraṇyagarbhas, or yogis, and as Bhagavān by the devotees. In other words, Bhagavān, or the Personality of Godhead, is the last word in the Absolute Truth, Paramātmā is the partial representation of the Personality of Godhead, and the impersonal Brahman is the glowing effulgence of the Personality of Godhead, as the sun rays are to the sun-god. Less intelligent students of either of the latter two schools sometimes argue in favor of their own realization, but those who are perfect seers of the Absolute Truth know well that the above three features of the one Absolute

Truth are different views seen from different angles of vision.

As explained in the first verse of the First Chapter of the *Bhāgavatam,* the Supreme Truth is self-sufficient, cognizant, and free from the illusion of relativity. In the relative world the knower is different from the known, but in the Absolute Truth the knower and the known are one and the same thing. In the relative world the knower is the living spirit, or superior energy, whereas the known is inert matter, or inferior energy. Therefore, there is a duality of inferior and superior energy, whereas in the absolute realm the knower and the known are of the same superior energy. There are th oned, thinking he belongs to the inferior energy. Therefore there is the sense of relativity in the material world. In the Absolute there is no such sense of difference between the knower and the known, and therefore everything there is absolute.

As mentioned above, the analogy of the sun and the sunshine is helpful for understanding Brahman, Paramātmā, and Bhagavān, the three aspects of the Absolute Truth. In one sense there is no difference between these three terms, just as there is in one sense no difference between the sunshine, the sun globe, and the sun-god, Vivasvān. All of them are light. The inhabitants of the sun globe, led by Vivasvān, possess bodies made of fire, and therefore everything on the sun is glowing. From a great distance we see the sun as a glowing globe, and the sunshine is the glow.

So, Brahman is like the sunshine, Paramātmā like the localized sun globe, and Bhagavān like the sun-god. They are one in the sense that they are all the pure light of the Absolute Truth, but still there is a difference: If you stand in the sunshine, that does not mean you have reached the sun globe or seen the predominating deity of the sun, Vivasvān. Similarly, the different means for understanding the Absolute Truth produce different realizations. One who tries to understand the Absolute simply by mental speculation may ultimately realize the impersonal Brahman, and one who tries to understand the Absolute through meditative yoga practice may be able to realize Paramātmā, but one who practices *bhakti-yoga* can achieve complete understanding of the Absolute Truth and realize the spiritual form of Bhagavān, the Personality of Godhead, who is the original source of everything.

There are many philosophers who are trying to find the original source of everything. The scientists are also trying to find that original source. They have concluded that everything originates from matter—this is the modern theory of chemical evolution. But although the theory of the so-called scientists is that everything, including life, comes from matter, they have not been able to produce life from chemicals.

The *Vedānta-sūtra* instructs that we *should* search out the original source of everything, the Absolute Truth. But the conclusion of all Vedic knowledge is that that source is a living being, not matter. As the *Kaṭha Upaniṣad* states, *nityo nityānāṁ cetanaś cetanānām eko bahūnāṁ yo vidadhāti kāmān:* "Among all the conscious living beings, there is one supreme living being, who is supplying all the others with their necessities." In the *Bhagavad-gītā* (10.8) Kṛṣṇa reveals that He is that supreme living being: *ahaṁ sarvasya prabhavo mattaḥ sarvaṁ pravartate.* "I am the source of everything." That *aham*—"I"—is Kṛṣṇa, the supreme living being, not dead matter. Similarly, earlier in the *Bhagavad-gītā* (7.7) Kṛṣṇa says,

mattaḥ parataraṁ nānyat kiñcid asti dhanañjaya
mayi sarvam idaṁ protaṁ sūtre maṇi-gaṇā iva

"O conqueror of wealth, there is no truth superior to Me. Everything rests upon Me, as pearls are strung on a thread."

So, we should understand that Kṛṣṇa, Bhagavān, is the last word in the Absolute Truth. In the *Bhagavad-gītā* (14.27) Kṛṣṇa states that the impersonal Brahman rests upon Him (*brahmaṇo hi pratiṣṭhāham*). Just as the sunshine comes from the sun, the light of Brahman that spreads throughout the universe comes from Kṛṣṇa. That is explained in the *Brahma-saṁhitā* (5.40):

yasya prabhā prabhavato jagad-aṇḍa-koṭi-
koṭiṣv aśeṣa-vasudhādi vibhūti-bhinnam

tad brahma niṣkalaṁ anantam aśeṣa-bhūtaṁ
govindam ādi-puruṣaṁ tam ahaṁ bhajāmi

The Brahman effulgence is Kṛṣṇa's bodily glow, known as the *brahmajyoti,* and this material world is generated out of that effulgence. In the *Bhagavad-gītā* (9.4) Kṛṣṇa says, *mayā tatam idaṁ sarvaṁ jagad avyakta-mūrtinā:* "My impersonal feature, the Brahman effulgence, is expanded everywhere." *Mat-sthāni sarva-bhūtāni:* "Everything is resting on that Brahman effulgence." *Na cāhaṁ teṣv avasthitaḥ:* "But I personally am not there." This is *tattva-jñāna,* knowledge of the Absolute Truth.

If we try to understand the Absolute Truth by dint of our speculative strength, then we can at most approach only up to the impersonal feature, just as if we try to understand the sun by our personal strength we can at most see the sunshine. But if we want to study the sun globe or understand the predominating deity of the sun, that is a different thing. For that, simply coming into the sunshine will not help you: you'll need some process by which you can go to the sun globe and meet the sun-god. Similarly, you can understand the impersonal Brahman by dint of your speculative knowledge, but you cannot understand the Paramātmā, the expansion of the Lord situated in everyone's heart, or Bhagavan, the Supreme Personality of Godhead and the origin of Brahman and Paramātmā.

The fact is that knowledge of Kṛṣṇa, Bhagavān, includes everything. Therefore the *Vedas* say, *kasmin tu bhagavo vijñāte sarvam idaṁ vijñātaṁ bhavati.* If you simply understand Kṛṣṇa, you will automatically understand the Brahman feature and the Paramātmā feature. You don't need to try to understand Brahman and Paramātmā separately: simply by understanding Kṛṣṇa, you will understand both.

Here is another example: Suppose you see a mountain from a great distance. You will simply see some cloudy, vague shape. But if you approach the mountain, you will see the same mountain much more distinctly, with its greenish color and massive form. And if you actually climb the mountain, you will find so many animals, men, houses, trees, and so on. The object is the same, but it appears different from different angles of vision.

So understanding Kṛṣṇa means understanding Brahman and Paramātmā as well, but we must understand Kṛṣṇa in truth. As He says in the *Bhagavad-gītā* (4.9),

> *janma karma ca me divyam evaṁ yo vetti tattvataḥ*
> *tyaktvā dehaṁ punar janma naiti mām eti so 'rjuna*

"One who knows the transcendental nature of My appearance and activities does not, upon leaving the body, take his birth again in this material world, but attains My eternal abode, O Arjuna." Here the word *tattvataḥ,* "in truth," is used." Because we do not make the effort to understand Kṛṣṇa in truth, we consider Him an ordinary human being. This is the way of the fools and rascals (*avajānanti māṁ mūḍhāḥ*). But Kṛṣṇa is not of this material world. Whoever actually understands Kṛṣṇa as the Absolute Truth has completed his mission in life, and at the end of this life he doesn't take birth again in this world but returns home, back to Godhead.

How to achieve that understanding is explained in the next verse.

7
Seeing God Within

tac chraddadhānā munayo
jñāna-vairāgya-yuktayā
paśyanty ātmani cātmānaṁ
bhaktyā śruta-gṛhītayā

The seriously inquisitive student or sage, well equipped with knowledge and detachment, realizes that Absolute Truth by rendering devotional service in terms of what he has heard from the Vedānta-śruti.

Śrīmad-Bhāgavatam 1.2.12

The Absolute Truth is realized in full by the process of devotional service to the Lord, Vāsudeva, or the Personality of Godhead, who is the full-fledged Absolute Truth. Brahman is His transcendental bodily effulgence, and Paramātmā is His partial representation. As such, Brahman or Paramātmā realization of the Absolute Truth is but a partial realization. There are four different types of human beings—the *karmīs,* the *jñānīs,* the yogis, and the devotees. The *karmīs* are materialistic, whereas the other three are transcendental. The first-class transcendentalists are the devotees who have realized the Supreme Person. The second-class transcendentalists are those who have partially realized the plenary portion of the absolute person. And the third-class transcendentalists are those who have barely realized the spiritual focus of the absolute person.

As stated in the *Bhagavad-gītā* and other Vedic literatures, the Supreme Person is realized by devotional service which is backed by full knowledge and detachment from material association. We have already discussed the point that devotional service is followed by knowledge and detachment from material association. As Brahman and Paramātmā realization are imperfect realizations of the Absolute Truth, so the means of realizing Brahman and Paramātmā, i.e., the paths of *jñāna* and yoga, are also imperfect means of realizing the Absolute Truth. Devotional service which is based on the foreground of full knowledge combined with detachment from material association and which is fixed by the aural reception of the Vedānta-śruti is the only perfect method by which the seriously inquisitive student can realize the Absolute Truth.

Devotional service is not, therefore, meant for the less intelligent class of transcendentalist. There are three classes of devotees, namely first, second, and third class. The third-class devotees, or the neophytes, who have no knowledge and are not detached from material association but who are simply attracted by the preliminary process of worshiping the Deity in the temple, are called material devotees. Material devotees are more attached to material benefit than transcendental profit. Therefore, one has to make definite progress from the position of material devotional service to the second-class devotional position. In the second-class position, the devotee can see four principles in the devotional line, namely the Personality of Godhead, His devotees, the ignorant, and the envious. One has to raise himself at least to the stage of a second-class devotee and thus become eligible to know the Absolute Truth.

A third-class devotee, therefore, has to receive the instructions of devotional service from the authoritative sources of *Bhāgavata*. The number one *Bhāgavata* is the established personality of devotee, and the other *Bhāgavata* is the message of Godhead. The third-class devotee therefore has to go to the personality of devotee in order to learn the instructions of devotional service. Such a personality of devotee is not a professional man who earns his livelihood by the business of the *Bhāgavatam.* Such a devotee must be a representative of Śukadeva Gosvāmī, like Sūta Gosvāmī, and must preach the cult of devotional service for the all-around benefit of all people. A neophyte devotee has very little taste for hearing from the authorities. Such a neophyte devotee makes a show of hearing from the professional man to satisfy his senses. This sort of hearing and chanting has spoiled the whole thing, so one should be very careful about the faulty process. The holy messages of Godhead, as inculcated in the *Bhagavad-gītā* or the *Śrīmad-Bhāgavatam,* are undoubtedly transcendental subjects, but even though they are so, such transcendental matters are not to be received from the professional man, who spoils them as the serpent spoils milk simply by the touch of his tongue.

A sincere devotee must therefore be prepared to hear the Vedic literature like the *Upaniṣads, Vedānta,* and other literatures left by the previous authorities, or Gosvāmīs, for the benefit of his progress. Without hearing such literatures, one cannot make actual progress. And without hearing and following the instructions, the show of devotional service becomes worthless and therefore a sort of disturbance in the path of devotional service. Unless, therefore, devotional service is established on the principles of *śruti, smṛti, purāṇa,* and *pañcarātra* authorities, the make-show of devotional service should at once be rejected. An unauthorized devotee should never be recognized as a pure devotee. By assimilation of such messages from the Vedic literatures, one can see the all-pervading localized aspect of the Personality of Godhead within his own self constantly. This is called *samādhi.*

Here the *Śrīmad-Bhāgavatam* states that the first requirement for achieving *samādhi* is *śraddhā,* faith. The *Caitanya-caritāmṛta* (*Madhya* 22.62) defines *śraddhā* as follows:

> *'śraddhā'-śabde——viśvāsa kahe sudṛḍha niścaya*
> *kṛṣṇe bhakti kaile sarva-karma kṛta haya*

When you firmly believe that by becoming a devotee of Kṛṣṇa

you will achieve all perfection, that is *śraddhā,* genuine faith. At the end of the *Bhagavad-gītā* (18.66), Kṛṣṇa says,

> *sarva-dharmān parityajya mām ekaṁ śaraṇaṁ vraja*
> *ahaṁ tvāṁ sarva-pāpebhyo mokṣayiṣyāmi mā śucaḥ*

"Voluntarily surrender unto Me and I will take charge of you. I will protect you from all sinful reactions; do not worry." When one accepts this instruction and surrenders to Kṛṣṇa immediately, without consideration, that is *śraddhā*. When you have such faith and you surrender to Kṛṣṇa, you become a *muni* or *mahātmā,* a great-minded soul endowed with knowledge and detachment (*tac chraddadhānā munayo jñāna-vairāgya-yuktayā*). The aim of human life is to acquire knowledge and detachment. Knowledge alone is useless; one must also have detachment. Therefore Śrīpāda Śaṅkarācārya, the founder of the Māyāvāda school, told his followers, "First become a *sannyāsī* [renunciant]; then you can speak." So one who is a actually a *jñānī,* a wise man, must also be a *vairāgī,* one who has given up all attachment to material things. And the result of this faith, surrender, knowledge, and detachment is *paśyanty ātmani cātmānam:* one sees the Paramātmā, the Supreme Soul, within his mind and within his self. This is confirmed elsewhere in the *Śrīmad-Bhāgavatam* (12.13.1): *dhyānāvasthita-tad-gatena manasā paśyanti yaṁ yoginaḥ.* "The perfect yogi always sees the Supreme Personality of Godhead within himself."

The perfect yogi has *prema,* pure love for Kṛṣṇa. As the *Brahma-saṁhitā* (5.38) states, *premāñjana-cchurita-bhakti-vilocanena santaḥ sadaiva hṛdayeṣu vilokayanti:* "The devotee who has anointed his eyes with the ointment of love of God always sees the beautiful blackish form of Kṛṣṇa within his heart." We cannot imagine how beautiful Kṛṣṇa is. It is said that His body is more beautiful than millions of Cupids (*kandarpa-koṭi-kamanīya-viśeṣa-śobhaṁ*). Cupid is very beautiful, but even if you place millions of Cupids together, their beauty cannot compare with Kṛṣṇa's. These things cannot be understood unless one's eyes are smeared with the ointment of love of Godhead.

We cannot understand God with our present blunt material senses, which are simply after material gratification. With them how can we perceive Kṛṣṇa, who is completely spiritual? It is not possible. Therefore we must purify the senses through the process of *bhakti:*

ataḥ śrī-kṛṣṇa-nāmādi na bhaved grāhyam indriyaiḥ
sevonmukhe hi jihvādau svayam eva sphuraty adaḥ

"No one can understand the transcendental nature of the name, form, qualities, and pastimes of Śrī Kṛṣṇa through his materially contaminated senses. Only when one becomes spiritually saturated by transcendental service to the Lord are the transcendental name, form, qualities, and pastimes of the Lord revealed to him" (*Bhakti-rasāmṛta-sindhu* 1.2.234).

Engaging in the service to the Lord helps one come to the platform of knowledge (*jñāna*) and detachment (*vairāgya*). One is in knowledge who understands, *ahaṁ brahmāsmi:* "I am not this material body; I am spirit soul." Now we have designated ourselves on the basis of our bodily relationships. We think, "I am an American," "I am an Indian," "I am a *brāhmaṇa,*" "I am black," "I am white," "I am strong," "I am weak," "I am fat," "I am thin." These are all bodily designations. When one becomes free of these designations and thinks, "I am an eternal servant of Kṛṣṇa," one possesses real *jñāna,* or knowledge.

As mentioned earlier, when one engages in devotional service to Kṛṣṇa, knowledge and detachment automatically come. But, as the present verse states, one must perform that devotional service by following the injunctions of the Vedic literatures. Śrīla Rūpa Gosvāmī confirms this in his *Bhakti-rasāmṛta-sindhu* (1.2.101),

śruti-smṛti-purāṇādi-pañcarātra-vidhiṁ vinā
aikāntikī harer bhaktir utpātāyaiva kalpate

"Devotional service of the Lord that ignores such authorized

Vedic literatures as the *Upaniṣads, Purāṇas,* and *Nārada-pañcarātra* is simply a disturbance in society."

These books have to be received through the channel of the disciplic succession (*paramparā*). In other words, to learn the science of *bhakti* one must accept a guru coming in disciplic succession from Kṛṣṇa. To understand the *Bhagavad-gītā,* for example, one should accept it just as Arjuna did—from Kṛṣṇa or his representative, in a mood of submission and service. Arjuna is part of the disciplic succession. Because the disciplic succession had been broken and the knowledge of the *Bhagavad-gītā* had been lost, Kṛṣṇa spoke the *Bhagavad-gītā* again to Arjuna. So, if you understand the *Bhagavad-gītā* and Kṛṣṇa as Arjuna understood them, your understanding will be perfect. But if you invent some imaginary meaning of the *Bhagavad-gītā*, you are wasting your time.

Don't waste your time. Try to understand Kṛṣṇa as He is, as He describes Himself in the *Bhagavad-gītā*. If God says, "I am like this," why are you wasting your time manufacturing ways and means to understand God differently? Kṛṣṇa is canvassing you: "I am God. Here is My name, here is My address, here are My activities." Everything is provided. Why don't you understand God from God? Why are you manufacturing your own ways to understand Him?

The Kṛṣṇa consciousness movement is not presenting some manufactured way to understand God. It is simply presenting the standard way. In the *Bhagavad-gītā* Kṛṣṇa says, *man-manā bhava mad-bhakto mad-yājī māṁ namaskuru:* "Think of Me, become My devotee, worship Me, and bow down before Me." And we are teaching the same thing. It is not difficult to follow this process. Anyone can do it. Sometimes people say that I have done something wonderful by spreading the Kṛṣṇa consciousness movement all over the world. But all I have done is present Kṛṣṇa as He is. That is the secret. So, anyone can understand Kṛṣṇa as He is from the *Bhagavad-gītā* and *Śrīmad-Bhāgavatam* and make his life perfect. Otherwise, any process you may invent for understanding God is simply a useless waste of time.

8

The Perfect Social Order

. . . . . .

ataḥ pumbhir dvija-śreṣṭhā
varṇāśrama-vibhāgaśaḥ
svanuṣṭhitasya dharmasya
saṁsiddhir hari-toṣaṇam

O best among the twice-born, it is therefore concluded that the highest perfection one can achieve by discharging the duties prescribed for one's own occupation according to caste divisions and orders of life is to please the Personality of Godhead.

Śrīmad-Bhāgavatam 1.2.13

Human society all over the world is divided into four castes and four orders of life. The four castes are the intelligent caste, the martial caste, the productive caste, and the laborer caste. These castes are classified in terms of one's work and qualification and not by birth. Then again there are four orders of life, namely the student life, the householder's life, the retired life, and the devotional life. In the best interest of human society there must be such divisions of life; otherwise no social institution can grow in a healthy state. And in each and every one of the above-mentioned divisions of life, the aim must be to please the supreme authority of the Personality of Godhead.

This institutional function of human society is known as the system of *varṇāśrama-dharma,* which is quite natural for the civilized life. The *varṇāśrama* institution is constructed to enable one to realize the Absolute Truth. It is not for artificial domination of one division over another. When the aim of life, i.e., realization of the Absolute Truth, is missed by too much attachment for *indriya-prīti,* or sense gratification, as already discussed hereinbefore, the institution of the *varṇāśrama* is utilized by selfish men to pose an artificial predominance over the weaker section. In the Kali-yuga, or the age of quarrel, this artificial predominance is already current, but the saner section of the people know it well that the divisions of castes and orders of life are meant for smooth social intercourse and high-thinking self-realization and not for any other purpose.

Herein the statement of the *Bhāgavatam* is that the highest aim of life, or the highest perfection of the institution of *varṇāśrama-dharma,* is to cooperate jointly for the satisfaction of the Supreme Lord. This is confirmed in the *Bhagavad-gītā* (4.13).

Here Sūta Gosvāmī addresses his audience with the word *dvija-śreṣṭhāḥ,* "O best of the *brāhmaṇas.*" This indicates that they are devotees of Kṛṣṇa and the best of learned scholars. In this age everyone is born a *śūdra,* a fourth-class man (*janmanā jāyate śūdraḥ*). By reformatory practices one can become a third-class man—a *dvija* (*saṁskārād bhaved dvijaḥ).* By cultivation of knowledge and culture, one becomes a second-class man, a *vipra* (*veda-pāṭhād bhaved vipraḥ*). But only one who knows Brahman is a first-class man, a *brāhmaṇa* (*brahma jānātīti brāhmaṇa*). And because the sages at Naimiṣāraṇya are the best of the *brāhmaṇas,* they know not only Brahman but Bhagavān, the Supreme Personality of Godhead.

The brahminical class is essential for actual human civilization, which begins with the social system of *varṇāśrama-dharma,* four *varṇas* and four *āśramas.* The four *varṇas* are the *brāhmaṇas* (the priests and intellectuals), the *kṣatriyas* (the warriors and administrators), the *vaiśyas* (the farmers and merchants), and the *śūdras* (the manual laborers). The four *āśramas* are the *brahmacārīs* (the celibate students), the *gṛhasthas* (the householders), the *vānaprasthas* (the retirees), and the *sannyāsīs* (the renunciants). Unless human society is scientifically organized according to this *varṇāśrama* system, it is animal society. It is not human society. And in animal society you cannot expect any intelligence or any sense of goodness or any idea of God. It is not possible.

The system of *varṇāśrama* is natural because it is a creation of God. Just as the body has four divisions—the brain, arms, belly, and legs—society also has four divisions—the *brāhmaṇas, kṣatriyas, vaiśyas,* and *śūdras*. This is natural. But if the head is cut off, what use is the body? It is a dead body. Similarly, at the present moment there is no brahminical culture in society, and so it is headless. There may be a very strong arm department (the *kṣatriyas*), a well-equipped economic department (the *vaiśyas*), and a numerous labor department (the *śūdras*), but because there is no head department (the *brāhmaṇas*), society is like a dead body. Therefore everyone is suffering.

In the Kṛṣṇa consciousness movement we are training *brāhmaṇas* so that human society may be saved. It is not that the other classes are unimportant. In the body the brain is very important, but the legs are also important because if your legs do not work and you cannot move, your brain cannot help you. So there must be cooperation between all the bodily limbs. Although the brain is the most important part of the body, still the legs are required, the hands are required, the belly is required—everything is required. Similarly, all the social and spiritual classes in the *varṇāśrama* system are necessary for society to function properly.

So, we do not disregard any social division, but we say that everyone must work for the satisfaction of Kṛṣṇa: *saṁsiddhir hari-toṣaṇam*. Then every member of society can achieve perfection. It doesn't matter what you do, but if you can satisfy Kṛṣṇa by your art and intelligence and education—in other words, by your work—then your life is perfect. We don't say, "Don't do your work." Do your work, but do it for Kṛṣṇa; then it is perfect. Otherwise, go to hell: *śrama eva hi kevalam.*

Someone may claim, "Oh, I am a philosopher, and I am doing my duty."

"But do you know God, and do you serve God?"

"Yes, I know God: I am God."

Such nonsense will not help you. Suppose an ordinary man claims, "I am the President of the United States." Everyone will understand he is a crazy fellow. Similarly, when a rascal says "I am God," we should understand he is crazy.

You have to satisfy the Supreme Lord with your service, not try to imitate Him. In the *Bhagavad-gītā* Kṛṣṇa never advises that you should claim to be Him. No. He says, *sarva-dharmān parityajya mām ekaṁ śaraṇaṁ vraja:* "Come under My shelter exclusively." He never says, "Become equal with Me." That is nonsense. Kṛṣṇa will be satisfied with you when you surrender to Him and try to serve Him, not when you falsely claim, "I am Kṛṣṇa," or "Kṛṣṇa is now dead and I have become God," or "There is no God." Such rascaldom will never satisfy Kṛṣṇa.

So, the instruction of the *Bhāgavatam* is *svanuṣṭhitasya dharmasya saṁsiddhir hari-toṣaṇam:* "Your perfection will come when you perform your duties nicely for the satisfaction of Hari, or Kṛṣṇa." The activities in the four social and four spiritual orders of the *varṇāśrama* system may sometimes appear material, but when they are performed for the satisfaction of Kṛṣṇa, they are no longer material; they are spiritual. "Material" simply means forgetfulness of Kṛṣṇa, that's all. Otherwise, there is nothing material. Those who are not thoroughly Kṛṣṇa conscious distinguish between material and spiritual, but when you are fully Kṛṣṇa conscious you see the oneness of everything, *ekatvam anupaśyataḥ* (*Īśopaniṣad* 7). This means that you see how everything is related to Kṛṣṇa.

Kṛṣṇa is the Supreme, and everything is an emanation of His energy, which is variegated. A good example is the sun: from the sun emanates the sunshine, which is made up of two energies—heat and light. The whole material creation is based on this heat and light. If there were no heat and light from the sun, the trees would quickly become skeletons. So, while we can distinguish between the sun's heat energy and light energy, in a higher sense they are one because they are both part of the sunshine.

Similarly, two basic energies of Kṛṣṇa are acting in this

world—His material energy and His spiritual energy. The material energy consists of earth, water, fire, air, ether, mind, intelligence, and ego, and the spiritual energy consists of the living entities (*jīva-bhūtāṁ mahā-bāho yayedaṁ dhāryate jagat*). So the material world is a combination of Kṛṣṇa's spiritual and material energies. And because 99.9% of the living entities here have forgotten God, here there is a distinction between the material and spiritual energies. But as soon as you advance in spiritual knowledge and become Kṛṣṇa conscious, you will no longer see anything as material; you will see that everything is spiritual: *sarvaṁ khalv idaṁ brahma*. As Śrī Caitanya Mahāprabhu says in the *Caitanya-caritāmṛta* (*Madhya* 8.274),

sthāvara-jaṅgama dekhe, nā dekhe tāra mūrti
sarvatra haya nija iṣṭa-deva-sphūrti

"A spiritually advanced, Kṛṣṇa conscious person sees all moving and nonmoving things, but he does not exactly see their forms. Rather, wherever he looks he sees the manifestation of His worshipable Lord." The vision of an atheist is just the opposite: even if he comes into the temple and sees the Deity form of Kṛṣṇa, he will simply see stone. But a spiritually advanced person who looks at the Deity will see Kṛṣṇa personally. When Caitanya Mahāprabhu entered the temple in Purī and saw the Deity of Jagannātha, He immediately exclaimed, "Here is My Kṛṣṇa!" and fainted.

So, to overcome our forgetfulness of Kṛṣṇa, we should make satisfying Him our only business (*saṁsiddhir hari-toṣanam*). And if your aim is simply to satisfy Kṛṣṇa, then your life is perfect.

9

The Sure Way to Know God

. . . . . .

tasmād ekena manasā
bhagavān sātvatāṁ patiḥ
śrotavyaḥ kīrtitavyaś ca
dhyeyaḥ pūjyaś ca nityadā

Therefore, with one-pointed attention one should constantly hear about, glorify, remember, and worship the Personality of Godhead, who is the protector of the devotees.

Śrīmad-Bhāgavatam 1.2.14

If realization of the Absolute Truth is the ultimate aim of life, it must be carried out by all means. In any one of the above-mentioned castes and orders of life, the four processes, namely glorifying, hearing, remembering, and worshiping, are general occupations. Without these principles of life, no one can exist. Activities of the living being involve engagements in these four different principles of life. Especially in modern society, all activities are more or less dependent on hearing and glorifying. Any man from any social status becomes a well-known man in human society within a very short time if he is simply glorified truly or falsely in the daily newspapers. Sometimes political leaders of a particular party are also advertised by newspaper propaganda, and by such a method of glorification an insignificant man becomes an important man—within no time.

But such propaganda by false glorification of an unqualified person cannot bring about any good, either for the particular man or for the society. There may be some temporary reactions to such propaganda, but there are no permanent effects. Therefore such activities are a waste of time. The actual object of glorification is the Supreme Personality of Godhead, who has created everything manifested before us. The tendency to glorify others or hear others glorified must be turned to the real object of glorification—the Supreme Being. And that will bring happiness.

Real satisfaction comes when you satisfy the Supreme Lord. And how should that be done? First by fixing the mind on Him with one-pointed attention (*ekena manasā*). You should not divert your attention to so many things but simply fix your mind on the Supreme Lord, Bhagavān. Previously the *Bhāgavatam* taught that the Absolute Truth is known as Brahman (the Lord's impersonal effulgence), Paramātmā (the Supersoul), and Bhagavān (the Personality of Godhead). But when it comes to focusing one's attention on the Absolute, one must focus on the Supreme Personality of Godhead, Lord Kṛṣṇa. Otherwise, how can we focus our attention? It is very difficult to fix the mind on the impersonal feature or the Supersoul. One can understand the impersonal Absolute Truth by philosophical speculation and the Supersoul by meditation, but both these processes are very difficult. Fixing the mind on Bhagavān, however, is easy and practical.

We can easily fix the mind on Kṛṣṇa by seeing His form in the temple, reading His instructions in the *Bhagavad-gītā,* hearing and chanting His holy names, and in so many other ways. There is no difficulty. But if you try to absorb your mind in the impersonal Brahman or the Supersoul, it is very difficult. As Kṛṣṇa says in the *Bhagavad-gītā* (12.5), *kleśo 'dhikataras teṣām avyaktāsakta-cetasām:* "For those who are attached to the impersonal feature of the Absolute Truth, advancement is very troublesome." For devotees of Kṛṣṇa, on the other hand, there is the joyful process of chanting the Hare Kṛṣṇa mantra, dancing in ecstasy, and eating sumptuous *kṛṣṇa-prasādam.*

And even if you follow the very troublesome path of impersonal realization for many, many lifetimes, working so hard to separate spirit from matter by the speculative process of *neti neti*—"This is not Brahman. This is not Brahman"— you'll still have to surrender to Kṛṣṇa if you want to achieve success: *bahūnāṁ janmanām ante jñānavān māṁ prapadyate*.

Now, one may say, "There are so many Bhagavāns. I can fix my mind on any of them." Nowadays people have manufactured many "Bhagavāns." But here the *Bhāgavatam* says *bhagavān sātvatāṁ patiḥ:* "You have to fix your mind on that Bhagavān whom the devotees accept as their Lord." There may be many Bhagavāns, but only the Supreme Personality of Godhead, Kṛṣṇa, is accepted as the Lord by all the stalwart devotees, *ācāryas,* and teachers, such as Brahmā and Śiva. The public may accept an ordinary man as Bhagavān and declare, "Here is an incarnation of God," but that is foolishness. Kṛṣṇa is God, as He Himself declares in the *Bhagavad-gītā* (7.7, 10.8). *Mattaḥ parataraṁ nānyat:* "There is nothing beyond Me." *Ahaṁ sarvasya prabhavaḥ:* "I am the origin of everything." *Mattaḥ sarvaṁ pravartate:* "Everything emanates from Me." *Iti matvā bhajante māṁ budhā bhāva-samanvitāḥ:* "Those who are actually learned know that I am the source of everything, and therefore they become My devotees."

The *Brahma-saṁhitā* (5.1) also states,

> *īśvaraḥ paramaḥ kṛṣṇaḥ sac-cid-ānanda-vigrahaḥ*
> *anādir ādir govindaḥ sarva-kāraṇa-kāraṇam*

"The Supreme God is Kṛṣṇa, who has an eternal form of bliss and knowledge." There are many gods, or controllers, but Kṛṣṇa is the Supreme God. Nobody is above Him. Therefore He is *anādi,* without origin. We all have an origin, but He has none because He is the origin of all (*ādiḥ*). He is known as Govinda because He is the reservoir of all pleasure, and He is the cause of all causes (*sarva-kāraṇa-kāraṇam*).

Now one may ask, "How should I fix my mind on Bhagavān?"

The *Bhāgavatam* answers, *śrotavyaḥ:* "You have to hear about Him."

"From whom should I hear?"

The best person to hear from is Kṛṣṇa Himself, who kindly explains Himself in the *Bhagavad-gītā.* Suppose you want to know something about me. You can ask a friend, and he may say something or other about me. But when I explain myself to you, that is perfect. Similarly, if you want to know the Supreme Personality of Godhead, the best way is just to hear directly from Him. But if you reject this process and try to know God through speculation, you will fail because your senses and mind are imperfect.

Then the next process the *Bhāgavatam* recommends is chanting (*kīrtitavyaś ca*). If you simply hear about Kṛṣṇa but do not repeat what you have heard to others, you will not advance very quickly in your understanding of God. Whatever you hear or read you should explain to others. That is perfection. That is why we have established *Back to Godhead* magazine. Daily our students hear and read about Kṛṣṇa, and then they must be thoughtful and write something about the science of Kṛṣṇa consciousness. And naturally when one writes or speaks of Kṛṣṇa one must think of Him (*dheyaḥ*). Finally, the *Bhāgavatam* recommends worship of the Lord (*pūjyaḥ*). Therefore we require to regularly visit temples and worship the Deities residing there.

So the *Bhāgavatam* says that with one-pointed attention we should hear about the Lord, chant about Him, think of Him, and worship Him. And all this should be done *nityadā,* regularly. This is the process of *bhakti-yoga.* Anyone who adopts this process can understand the Absolute Truth. That is the clear declaration of this verse of the *Śrīmad-Bhāgavatam.*

10

The Sword of Remembrance

. . . .

yad-anudhyāsinā yuktāḥ
karma-granthi-nibandhanam
chindanti kovidās tasya
ko na kuryāt kathā-ratim

With sword in hand, intelligent men cut through the binding knots of reactionary work [karma] by remembering the Personality of Godhead. Therefore, who will not pay attention to His message?
Śrīmad-Bhāgavatam 1.2.15

The contact of the spiritual spark with material elements creates a knot which must be cut if one wants to be liberated from the actions and reactions of fruitive work. Liberation means freedom from the cycle of reactionary work. This liberation automatically follows for one who constantly remembers the transcendental pastimes of the Personality of Godhead. This is because all the activities of the Supreme Lord (His *līlā*) are transcendental to the modes of the material energy. They are all-attractive spiritual activities, and therefore constant association with the spiritual activities of the Supreme Lord gradually spiritualizes the conditioned soul and ultimately severs the knot of material bondage.

Liberation from material bondage is, therefore, a by-product of devotional service. Attainment of spiritual knowledge is not sufficient to insure liberation. Such knowledge must be overcoated with devotional service so that ultimately the devotional service alone predominates. Then liberation is made possible. Even the reactionary work of the fruitive workers can lead one to liberation when it is overcoated with devotional service. Karma overcoated with devotional service is called *karma-yoga*. Similarly, empirical knowledge overcoated with devotional service is called *jñāna-yoga*. But pure *bhakti-yoga* is independent of such karma and *jñāna* because it alone can not only endow one with liberation from conditional life but also award one the transcendental loving service of the Lord.

Therefore, any sensible man who is above the average man with a poor fund of knowledge must constantly remember the Personality of Godhead by hearing about Him, by glorifying Him, by remembering Him, and by worshiping Him always, without cessation. That is the perfect way of devotional service. The Gosvāmīs of Vṛndāvana, who were authorized by Śrī Caitanya Mahāprabhu to preach the *bhakti* cult, rigidly followed this rule and made immense literatures of transcendental science for our benefit. They have chalked out ways for all classes of men in terms of the different castes and orders of life in pursuance of the teachings of *Śrīmad-Bhāgavatam* and similar authoritative scriptures.

Unless we read, hear, and remember these literatures, we cannot cut the knot of our karmic reactions. Suppose a man is tied very strongly with ropes. With his hands and legs bound up, he cannot move independently. Similarly, we are tied up by the laws of material nature. The more sinful we are, the more the material nature binds us. For example, we are always bound by the laws of the state, either the criminal laws or the civil laws. If we violate the criminal laws, our punishment is very severe, and if we violate the civil laws, we are punished less severely—but in either case we are punished.

For the conditioned living entities in the material world, the body itself is a punishment. But people do not know this, and so they are trying to enjoy the body just like hogs. A village hog doesn't know how abominable it is that he has the body of hog and that he must eat stool and live in a filthy place. He is happy if he can simply enjoy sex with a female hog—never mind whether she is his sister, mother, or daughter. This is the hog's life—eating stool and enjoying sex. We are conscious of his abominable condition, but he is thinking, "Oh, what a happy life I have! I am dining very nicely on first-class food and having sex without any restriction. This is life."

Actually, this is *māyā,* illusion. *Māyā* has two energies, the *āvaraṇātmikā-śakti* and the *prakṣepātmikā-śakti.* The *āvaraṇātmikā-śakti* covers a living entity with ignorance. Even though he is living a condemned life, still he will think, "I am very happy. I am all right." His real knowledge is covered. And the *prakṣepātmikā-śakti* throws the living entity down into the ocean of material existence and keeps him there. When somebody is trying to come to Kṛṣṇa consciousness, the *prakṣepātmikā-śakti* will dictate, "Why are you going to the Kṛṣṇa consciousness society? There are so many restrictions there, so many rules and regulations. Better give it up." And the conditioned soul thinks, "Why, yes, this Kṛṣṇa consciousness is nonsense. Let me give it up."

The more sinful one is, the more *māyā* will prevent one from becoming Kṛṣṇa conscious. That is *māyā's* thankless task. She is just like the police department. The police are no one's enemy, but when someone commits a crime they arrest him, put him in jail, and punish him. Similarly, *māyā* is engaged by the supreme authority, Kṛṣṇa, to punish the sinful living entities.

So, the knot of the materialistic way of life is very strong, and the beginning of the knot is sex life. The whole world is bound up by the material laws of nature because of the strong desire for sex. Both in the human society and the animal society, the central point is sex. People are working so hard to earn money because they want to enjoy sex. Even the hippies could not give it up. They renounced everything—their father's property, their happy life at home—but sex they could not renounce.

Still, although the knot of material life is very difficult to cut, here the *Bhāgavatam* gives us the way: *yad-anudhyāsinā yuktāḥ karma-granthi-nibandhanam chindanti.* "With the sword of remembering Kṛṣṇa, you can cut the hard knot of material life." The best way to remember Kṛṣṇa is to always chant Hare Kṛṣṇa, Hare Kṛṣṇa, Kṛṣṇa Kṛṣṇa, Hare Hare/ Hare Rāma, Hare Rāma, Rāma Rāma, Hare Hare. Take this sword of chanting the *mahā-mantra;* in this age it is the only means for cutting the knot of material life.

Material life means *karma,* fruitive activities. By performing fruitive activities in this life a person creates his next body. One who acts sinfully may get a dog's body or a hog's body or a tree's body, and one who acts piously may get a demigod's body. But that is also a "knot"; it is not freedom, because even the demigods, the most materially advanced living beings in the universe, must die.

People are trying to be happy by becoming materially advanced. They do not know that the goal of life is to attain Kṛṣṇa consciousness (*na te viduḥ svārtha-gatiṁ hi viṣṇum*). They think, "By increasing motorcars, we shall be happy." This is *māyā,* illusion. Motorcars will not make you happy. This motorcar civilization will be finished within at most a hundred years. Anything we manufacture—a so-called empire, a so-called material civilization—will one day be finished. All these things simply constitute so many knots in the heart, captivating us and leading us to think, "What use is this Kṛṣṇa consciousness movement? We must have three dozen motorcars and three dozen wine bottles, and then we will be happy." This is illusion.

In the mood of someone bound up by illusion, Narottama dāsa Ṭhākura sings,

sat-saṅga chāḍi' kainu asate vilāsa
te-kāraṇe lāgila ye karma-bandha-phāṅsa

"Alas, I have given up the association of Kṛṣṇa's devotees because I wanted to enjoy illusory material happiness. In this way I have become entangled in the network of karma." Here Narottama uses the word *sat-saṅga,* meaning "association with devotees of Kṛṣṇa." *Sat-saṅga* can be found in the Kṛṣṇa consciousness movement, where one can hear the *Śrīmad-Bhāgavatam,* chant Hare Kṛṣṇa, and practice how to become pure. Just the opposite is *asat-saṅga,* bad association, which leads one to intoxication, illicit sex, drinking, and so many other sinful practices. The advertisers are *asat-saṅga:* "Come on, smoke Kool cigarettes and make your brain cool." The rascals! How can someone become cool by smoking cigarettes? By smoking fire one can become cool? Still, the advertisements are being presented, and the foolish people who are captivated by them smoke cigarettes to become cool. This is *māyā.*

One who is a little intelligent, however, will immediately see the contradiction in the advertisement: "This advertisement is claiming I can become cool by smoking cigarettes? What is this nonsense?" Similarly, an intelligent person can understand *māyā's* tricks and see the contradictions in all her allurements.

Therefore here the *Bhāgavatam* uses the word *kovida,* "intelligent person." When one actually becomes intelligent, he must ask, "Why am I in this miserable condition of life? I do not want to die, but death is there. Why? I do not want disease, but disease is there. Why? I do not want old age, but it is forced upon me. Why? I don't want war, but the draft board is dragging me to war. Why?" An intelligent person must ask all these "why" questions. Sanātana Gosvāmī showed the proper way to inquire from the guru when he approached Caitanya Mahāprabhu: *ke āmi, kene āmāya jāre tāpa-traya.* "Who am I?" asked Sanātana Gosvāmī. "Why have I been put into this miserable condition of life? My dear Lord, because I am the king's minister and I know a little Sanskrit and Arabic, the common people call me a *paṇḍita,* a learned scholar. But to tell You frankly, if I do not know what I am and why I am suffering, what is the value of my education?" This is intelligence.

Intelligence is shown by self-control. The cats and dogs have no self-control. If a bull or a male cat or dog sees a female, immediately he will rape her, yet he will not be punished. But if a human being does that on the street, he will be arrested at once. The inclination to rape is there in both the animal and the human being, but a human being is supposed to control himself.

Indeed, human life is *meant* for self-control. The more you control yourself, the more perfect a human being you become, and the more you allow your senses to run loose, the more of an animal you are. People do not know this. They want freedom, but in the name of freedom they are becoming animals. This is their so-called civilization.

So we have to follow the *Bhāgavatam's* instruction and become *kovida,* intelligent. An intelligent person should take up the sword of remembrance of Kṛṣṇa (*anudhyāsinā*) and cut the knot of attachment to material enjoyment. One meaning of the prefix *anu* in *anudhyāsinā* is "following." This indicates we should follow in the footsteps of a genuine spiritual master, or *ācārya.* What the *ācārya* is teaching and showing by his example, we should follow. Another meaning of *anu* is "always." We should always remember Kṛṣṇa if we want to cut the knot of karma binding us to birth and death in this material world.

It is the knot of karma that forces us to transmigrate from one body to another. This is not Darwin's theory of evolution—that nature causes a gradual evolution of bodies. Rather, each soul determines his future body by his actions in this life. The bodies are already there, and a living entity simply enters a particular type of body according to his karma. Suppose I act so abominably in this life that in my next life I must suffer the punishment of becoming a dog. Then I'll have to enter the womb of a female dog, and she will give me the body of dog. Eventually I will come out and experience life in a dog's body. This is the law of karma.

So you can become dog, or you can become a god. As a human being you have the facility to become either. You simply have to choose. As Kṛṣṇa says in the *Bhagavad-gītā* (9.25),

> *yānti deva-vratā devān pitṝn yānti pitṛ-vratāḥ*
> *bhūtāni yānti bhūtejyā yānti mad-yājino 'pi mām*

"Those who worship the demigods will take birth among the demigods; those who worship the ancestors go to the ancestors; those who worship ghosts and spirits will take birth among such beings; and those who worship Me will live with Me." But if you want to live with God in the spiritual world you must have a body like His, just as if you want to live in the water you must have the body of a fish. And if you don't want to live with God, if you want to enjoy unrestricted sense enjoyment, then you can take the body of a hog. Nature gives the chance to every human being to select his own future; no one is forced.

Therefore one must be intelligent and inquire, "How can I be freed from material bondage?" The Supreme Personality of Godhead, Kṛṣṇa, answers this question in the *Bhagavad-gītā* (4.9):

janma karma ca me divyam evaṁ yo vetti tattvataḥ
tyaktvā dehaṁ punar janma naiti mām eti so 'rjuna

"One who knows the transcendental nature of My appearance and activities does not, upon leaving the body, take his birth again in this material world, but attains My eternal abode, O Arjuna." Here Kṛṣṇa says that one must know Him in truth, *tattvataḥ*. Such knowledge comes from authorized *śāstras* like the *Bhagavad-gītā* and *Śrīmad-Bhāgavatam*. But today so many rascals are advertising, "You don't need to understand God through any book. Just accept me as God." And people are so foolish that they accept such rascals as God.

Every claim in the scientific world is supported by some book. For example, suppose someone comes upon a tree and claims it is a mango tree. Then one can check the claim by referring to a book on botany and learning the characteristics of a mango tree—how its leaves are shaped, how its fruit tastes, and so on. The same is true in the fields of chemistry, physics, and every other science.

Similarly, there is a process for testing whether someone is God or not. When Caitanya Mahāprabhu was asked how to test if a person is God, He said, "The *śāstra* mentions the characteristics of God. If someone has those characteristics, He is God." So we are accepting Kṛṣṇa as God not on blind faith but because His character and activities are mentioned in the *śāstra*.

And we should use the same process to determine who is a genuine spiritual master: not by blind faith, but by reference to *śāstra*. About the genuine guru the *Śrīmad-Bhāgavatam* (11.3.21) says,

tasmād guruṁ prapadyeta jijñāsuḥ śreya uttamam
śābde pare ca niṣṇātaṁ brahmaṇy upaśamāśrayam

"A person who seriously desires real happiness must seek out a bona fide spiritual master and take shelter of him by initiation. The qualification of the bona fide guru is that he has realized the conclusions of the scriptures by deliberation and is able to convince others of these conclusions. Such great personalities, who have taken shelter of the Supreme Godhead, leaving aside all material considerations, should be understood to be bona fide spiritual masters."

So, one should be intelligent enough to take shelter of a bona fide guru. This will enable one to cut the hard knot of material life with the weapon of remembrance of Kṛṣṇa. It is not difficult. One simply has to cultivate an attraction for hearing about Kṛṣṇa (*kathā-ratim*). You don't need to pass an M.A. or Ph.D. examination. God has given you ears. Simply sit down and hear books like the *Śrīmad-Bhāgavatam* and *Bhagavad-gītā* from a realized person. These books contain everything you need to understand God. All you have to do is increase your attachment for hearing them. Simply by hearing repeatedly, you will become expert in the science of God. Caitanya Mahāprabhu has approved this process: *sthāne sthitāḥ śruti-gatāṁ tanu-vāṅ-manobhiḥ.* Remain in your social position, but try to hear the transcendental message from realized souls. You will gradually become enlightened and cut the knot of material bondage.

His Divine Grace A. C. Bhaktivedanta Swami Prabhupāda

The Founder-Ācārya of the International Society for Krishna Consciousness and the greatest exponent of Kṛṣṇa consciousness in the modern world.

PLATE ONE: Lord Caitanya (center, in gold), accompanied by His plenary expansion Nityānanda Prabhu (to Lord Caitanya's right, in blue), His incarnation Advaita Prabhu (to Nityānanda's left, with beard) and His pure devotees spread love of Godhead through the chanting of the Hare Kṛṣṇa *mantra*.

PLATE TWO: The material body is the cage of the soul, and if we simply care for the body, the soul will never become happy. (*p.* 4)

PLATE THREE: The atheists simply defy God, challenging "Where is your Kṛṣṇa? Where is God?" and in the end they also see Him, as death. (*p.* 13)

PLATE FOUR: We have been entangled in the materialistic way of life because of attachment. We live our life in ignorance, and after death we get another life, another body. (*p.* 17)

PLATE FIVE: Because the disciplic succession had been broken and the knowledge of the *Bhagavad-gītā* had been lost, Kṛṣṇa spoke the *Gītā* again to Arjuna. (*p.* 54)

PLATE SIX: By nature every living entity wants to enjoy life without work because that is what Kṛṣṇa is doing. Kṛṣṇa is always enjoying with Rādhārāṇī and the other *gopīs,* but He's not working. (*p.* 31)

11

Hearing of Kṛṣṇa With Faith

. . . .

śuśrūṣoḥ śraddadhānasya
vāsudeva-kathā-ruciḥ
syān mahat-sevayā viprāḥ
puṇya-tīrtha-niṣevaṇāt

O twice-born sages, by serving those devotees who are completely freed from all vice, great service is done. By such service, one gains affinity for hearing the messages of Vāsudeva.

Śrīmad-Bhāgavatam 1.2.16

The conditioned life of a living being is caused by his revolting against the Lord. There are men called *devas,* or godly living beings, and there are men called *asuras,* or demons, who are against the authority of the Supreme Lord. In the *Bhagavad-gītā* (Sixteenth Chapter) a vivid description of the *asuras* is given, in which it is said that the *asuras* are put into lower and lower states of ignorance life after life and so sink to the lower animal forms and have no information of the Absolute Truth, the Personality of Godhead. These *asuras* are gradually rectified to God consciousness by the mercy of the Lord's liberated servitors in different countries according to the supreme will. Such devotees of God are very confidential associates of the Lord, and when they come to save human society from the dangers of godlessness, they are known as powerful incarnations of the Lord, as sons of the Lord, as servants of the Lord, or as associates of the Lord. But none of them falsely claim to be God themselves. This is a blasphemy declared by the *asuras,* and the demoniac followers of such *asuras* also accept pretenders as God or His incarnation. In the revealed scriptures there is definite information of the incarnations of God. No one should be accepted as God or an incarnation of God unless he is confirmed by the revealed scriptures.

The servants of God are to be respected as God by the devotees who actually want to go back to Godhead. Such servants of God are called *mahātmās,* or *tīrthas,* and they preach according to particular time and place. The servants of God urge people to become devotees of the Lord. They never tolerate being called God. Śrī Caitanya Mahāprabhu was God Himself according to the indication of the revealed scriptures, but He played the part of a devotee. People who knew Him to be God addressed Him as God, but He used to block His ears with His hands and chant the name of Lord Viṣṇu. He strongly protested against being called God, although undoubtedly He was God Himself. The Lord behaves so to warn us against unscrupulous men who take pleasure in being addressed as God.

The servants of God come to propagate God consciousness, and intelligent people should cooperate with them in every respect. By serving the servant of God, one can please God more than by directly serving the Lord. The Lord is more pleased when He sees that His servants are properly respected because such servants risk everything for the service of the Lord and so are very dear to the Lord. The Lord declares in the *Bhagavad-gītā* (18.69) that no one is dearer to Him than one who risks everything to preach His glory. By serving the servants of the Lord, one gradually gets the quality of such servants, and thus one becomes qualified to hear the glories of God. The eagerness to hear about God is the first qualification of a devotee eligible for entering the kingdom of God.

As mentioned in this verse of the *Bhāgavatam,* such eagerness is awakened by rendering service to the *mahātmās,* or great souls. Who is a great soul? One who is engaged in the service of the Lord twenty-four hours a day. In the *Bhagavad-gītā* (9.13) Lord Kṛṣṇa describes the *mahātmā* in this way:

mahātmānas tu māṁ pārtha daivīṁ prakṛtim āśritāḥ
bhajanty ananya manaso jñātvā bhūtādim avyayam

"Those who are not deluded, the great souls, are under the protection of My divine nature. They are fully engaged in devotional service because they know Me as the Supreme Personality of Godhead, original and inexhaustible."

Here Kṛṣṇa uses the word *daivī-prakṛti,* "divine nature." In the *Bhagavad-gītā* Kṛṣṇa explains that He has two kinds of *prakṛtis,* or natures: the *daivī-* or *parā-prakṛti,* which is His transcendental nature, and the *aparā-prakṛti,* His material nature. Devotees of Kṛṣṇa try to remain under the guidance of *daivī-prakṛti* personified, Śrīmatī Rādhārāṇī. Materialists, however, are under the control of the *aparā-prakṛti,* personified as Goddess Kālī, or Durgā. So to develop our eagerness to hear about Kṛṣṇa (*vāsudeva-kathā-ruci*), we have to render service to a person who is under the protection and guidance of Kṛṣṇa's transcendental nature.

That service begins with faith (*śuśrūṣoḥ śraddadhānasya*). Without faith, you cannot make any progress. As Śrīla Rūpa Gosvāmī has written, *ādau śraddhā:* "The beginning of spiritual life is faith." That faith can be simply some appreciation for Kṛṣṇa consciousness. Without even taking up the process of *bhakti-yoga,* if a person thinks, "These Hare Kṛṣṇa people are very nice," such appreciation will give him a touch of spiritual life. And the development of this appreciation by degrees will be the development of his spiritual life.

The next stage is *sādhu-saṅga,* association with devotees of Kṛṣṇa. In this stage one may think, "All right, the devotees are chanting Hare Kṛṣṇa and talking of Kṛṣṇa. Let me go to the temple and sit down and hear." The third stage is *bhajana-kriyā,* beginning to perform the processes of devotional service. And after one has been associating nicely with devotees and engaging in devotional service for some time, chanting the Hare Kṛṣṇa *mantra* and observing the regulative principles, one will naturally feel, "Why not become a disciple of a spiritual master?" Therefore we receive many applications: "Śrīla Prabhupāda, kindly accept me as your disciple."

Then comes *anartha-nivṛtti,* vanquishing unwanted habits. One of these habits is illicit sex. We prohibit this in our Society. If one of our members wants to have sex, he or she can get married, but sex outside marriage is strictly forbidden. It is simply an *anartha,* rascaldom. Another *anartha* is intoxication. What is the use of intoxication? There is no need for it. In our Society we prohibit any kind of intoxication. We don't even allow coffee, tea, or cigarrettes. So, are we dying for want of tea or cigarrettes? No. Nor are we dying for want of meat-eating or gambling, which we also prohibit. Therefore all these things are *anarthas,* unnecessary things.

So the first stage in the development of a taste for hearing about Kṛṣṇa is some preliminary appreciation, the second stage is association with devotees, the third is engagement in devotional service, and the fourth stage—achieved if one is actually executing the rules and regulations of devotional service under the guidance of a bona fide spiritual master—is freedom from unwanted desires and habits. Then comes *niṣṭhā,* firm faith in the process of Kṛṣṇa consciousness. And the sixth stage is *ruci,* a taste for hearing and chanting about Kṛṣṇa, serving Him, and so on.

Suppose a person is suffering from jaundice. To him sugar candy tastes bitter, not sweet, but sugar candy is the best medicine for him. If he eats sugar candy, gradually his disease will be cured, and at last he will come to the point where candy tastes sweet again. Similarly, to come to the stage of *vāsudeva-kathā-ruci,* a taste for hearing the glorification of Kṛṣṇa, you must first go through the five stages mentioned above, which sometimes may appear bitter. But if you continually hear about Kṛṣṇa with faith and appreciation, you will surely come to the stage of tasting. Then you will get the sword of remembrance of Kṛṣṇa spoken of in the last verse, *yad anudhyāsinā.* If you have a taste for hearing and chanting about Kṛṣṇa, you can very easily remember Kṛṣṇa by constantly chanting Hare Kṛṣṇa, Hare Kṛṣṇa, Kṛṣṇa Kṛṣṇa, Hare Hare/ Hare Rāma, Hare Rāma, Rāma Rāma, Hare Hare.

So you have to take up the sword of Kṛṣṇa consciousness and cut the knot of material entanglement. The Kṛṣṇa consciousness movement is spreading by teaching people how to take up this sword. I started this movement in New York in 1966. I had no actual sword, like those wielded by some religious preachers. They take their scriptures in one hand and a sword in the other and say, "Accept this scripture or I'll cut off your head!" No, this is not the way of spreading Kṛṣṇa consciousness. Still, I did have a sword—the sword of remembrance of Kṛṣṇa—which I taught people to use by giving them a chance to hear about the Lord. The effect of hearing about the Lord is described in the next verse.

12

Cleansing the Heart By Hearing of God

. . . . . .

śṛṇvatāṁ sva-kathāḥ kṛṣṇaḥ
puṇya-śravaṇa-kīrtanaḥ
hṛdy antaḥ stho hy abhadrāṇi
vidhunoti suhṛt satām

Śrī Kṛṣṇa, the Personality of Godhead, who is the Paramātmā [Supersoul] in everyone's heart and the benefactor of the truthful devotee, cleanses desire for material enjoyment from the heart of the devotee who has developed the urge to hear His messages, which are in themselves virtuous when properly heard and chanted.

Śrīmad-Bhāgavatam 1.2.17

Messages of the Personality of Godhead Śrī Kṛṣṇa are nondifferent from Him. Whenever, therefore, offenseless hearing and glorification of God are undertaken, it is to be understood that Lord Kṛṣṇa is present there in the form of transcendental sound, which is as powerful as the Lord personally. Śrī Caitanya Mahāprabhu, in His *Śikṣāṣṭaka,* declares clearly that the holy name of the Lord has all the potencies of the Lord and that He has endowed His innumerable names with the same potency. There is no rigid fixture of time, and anyone can chant the holy name with attention and reverence at his convenience.

The Lord is so kind to us that He can be present before us personally in the form of transcendental sound, but unfortunately we have no taste for hearing and glorifying the Lord's name and activities. We have already discussed developing a taste for hearing and chanting the holy sound. It is done through the medium of service to the pure devotee of the Lord.

The Lord is reciprocally respondent to His devotees. When He sees that a devotee is completely sincere in getting admittance to the transcendental service of the Lord and has thus become eager to hear about Him, the Lord acts from within the devotee in such a way that the devotee may easily go back to Him. The Lord is more anxious to take us back into His kingdom than we can desire. Most of us do not desire at all to go back to Godhead. Only a very few men want to go back to Godhead. But anyone who desires to go back to Godhead, Śrī Kṛṣṇa helps in all respects.

One cannot enter into the kingdom of God unless one is perfectly cleared of all sins. The material sins are products of our desires to lord it over material nature. It is very difficult to get rid of such desires. Women and wealth are very difficult problems for the devotee making progress on the path back to Godhead. Many stalwarts in the devotional line fell victim to these allurements and thus retreated from the path of liberation. But when one is helped by the Lord Himself, the whole process becomes as easy as anything by the grace of the Lord.

To become restless in the contact of women and wealth is not an astonishment, because every living being is associated with such things from remote time, practically immemorial, and it takes time to recover from this foreign nature. But if one is engaged in hearing the glories of the Lord, gradually he realizes his real position. By the grace of God such a devotee gets sufficient strength to defend himself from the state of disturbances, and gradually all disturbing elements are eliminated from his mind.

Hearing the glories of Lord Kṛṣṇa is very easy because He has performed so many activities and these have been recorded extensively in authorized Vedic literatures like the *Mahā-*

bhārata and *Śrīmad-Bhāgavatam*. The *Bhāgavatam* is full of descriptions of Kṛṣṇa's pastimes, and besides being purifying to hear, they are very relishable also. People often take pleasure in reading fictional stories, but if you simply read *Śrīmad-Bhāgavatam* instead, you will relish that reading and at the same time become self-realized.

As Parīkṣit Mahārāja heard *Śrīmad-Bhāgavatam* he said, *nivṛtta-tarṣair upagīyamānād bhavauṣadhāc chrotra-mano-'bhirāmāt:* "Narrations about Kṛṣṇa are the proper medicine for those suffering in material existence, and such narrations are very relishable to hear, especially for those who are free of all material hankering."

As long as you are in material existence, you will feel hankering and lamenting because this world is being conducted chiefly by the modes of passion and ignorance. Therefore ordinarily we hanker to possess something, and if somehow or other we acquire that thing and it is lost, we lament. Hankering and lamenting and other effects of the lower modes of nature are known as *abhadrāṇi,* dirt within the heart. But in the present verse of the *Śrīmad-Bhāgavatam* Sūta Gosvāmī says that if you simply hear about Kṛṣṇa these dirty things will gradually be cleansed away from your heart by the Lord Himself.

So while Parīkṣit Mahārāja has said that narrations about Kṛṣṇa are especially relishable for persons who have transcended all hankering and lamenting, he also says that for the common man these narrations are *bhavauṣadhāc chrotra-mano-'bhirāmāt*—very pleasing to the ears and the heart, and the proper medicine to cure the disease of material life.

Therefore our program in the Kṛṣṇa consciousness society is to give people in general a chance to hear about Kṛṣṇa. This is our mission, which has been given to us by Caitanya Mahāprabhu. He said (Cc. *Madhya* 7.128):

yāre dekha, tāre kaha 'kṛṣṇa'-upadeśa
āmāra ājñāya guru hañā tāra' ei deśa

"On my order become a spiritual master and try to explain

kṛṣṇa-kathā to everyone you meet." *Kṛṣṇa-kathā* means words spoken by Kṛṣṇa, such as the *Bhagavad-gītā,* and words about Kṛṣṇa, such as the *Śrīmad-Bhāgavatam.* Caitanya Mahāprabhu ordered us to distribute these two kinds of *kṛṣṇa-kathā* throughout the whole world.

Now, one may ask me, "What is your qualification to be a spiritual master?" My qualification is that under the supreme order of Śrī Caitanya Mahāprabhu, coming down in disciplic succession, I am just trying to preach *kṛṣṇa-kathā.* That's all. I have not manufactured the process of Kṛṣṇa consciousness. No. I am simply a messenger, delivering Kṛṣṇa's message as it is. That's all. And the message is effective because I am not adulterating it. In the *Bhagavad-gītā* Kṛṣṇa says, *sarva-dharmān parityajya mām ekaṁ śaraṇaṁ vraja:* "Give up all your nonsense and just surrender unto Me." And I say the same thing: "Become a devotee of Kṛṣṇa. Surrender to Kṛṣṇa." So because I am not adulterating or misinterpreting Kṛṣṇa's message, there is no doubt that I am really representing His interests. Therefore the message is proving effective.

Before I came to the Western world, many others had come from India and taught the *Bhagavad-gītā.* Some of these teachers were great scholars. But because they did not deliver Kṛṣṇa's message as it is, no Westerners ever accepted the principles of *bhakti-yoga,* or Kṛṣṇa consciousness. Now the Westerners are accepting by the thousands, especially the youngsters. Many of them are no longer interested in material advancement. They have tasted it and are dissatisfied; now they are looking for spiritual advancement. They have come to the stage described at the beginning of the *Vedānta-sūtra: athāto brahma-jijñāsā.* "Now in this human form of life one should inquire into Brahman, the Absolute Truth." And when they inquire from us we immediately explain that, according to the *Bhagavad-gītā,* Kṛṣṇa is the Absolute Truth. As Arjuna declared when he understood who Kṛṣṇa was: *paraṁ brahma paraṁ dhāma pavitraṁ paramaṁ bhavān.* "You are the Supreme Personality of Godhead, the ultimate abode, the purest, the Absolute Truth." So when the inquiry into the Absolute

Truth comes, we can supply the *kṛṣṇa-kathā* to satisfy it.

Therefore everyone should join the Kṛṣṇa consciousness movement. One simply has to hear *kṛṣṇa-kathā* and distribute this knowledge, as ordered by Śrī Caitanya Mahāprabhu. The result will be what Sūta Gosvāmī describes here in the *Śrīmad-Bhāgavatam*: *śṛṇvatāṁ sva-kathāḥ kṛṣṇaḥ puṇya-śravaṇa-kīrtanaḥ. Kṛṣṇa-kathā* is so nice that just by hearing it one becomes pious. Even if one does not understand who Kṛṣṇa is, if one simply hears the vibration of the holy names—Hare Kṛṣṇa, Hare Kṛṣṇa, Kṛṣṇa Kṛṣṇa, Hare Hare/ Hare Rāma, Hare Rāma, Rāma Rāma, Hare Hare—one will become pious. *Kṛṣṇa-kathā* is so effective in polishing the heart, as Caitanya Mahāprabhu has said in His *Śikṣāṣṭaka: ceto-darpaṇa-mārjanam*. Kṛṣṇa is within our hearts as the Paramātmā, or Supersoul, and as soon as He understands that we are very seriously hearing about Him, He helps us by cleansing our hearts.

The exact word used here for the dirty things in our hearts is *abhadrāṇi,* "that which is ignoble." *Bhadra* means "noble," and *abhadra* means "ignoble." So, what is it that is ignoble within our hearts? Our claim to proprietorship over the property of God. A good example is nationalism, which many people today claim is so valuable. Nationalism is eulogized so much in the modern age, but actually it is most ignoble. How can we say this? On the strength of the *Īśopaniṣad* (Mantra 1):

īśāvāsyam idam sarvaṁ yat kiñca jagatyāṁ jagat
tena tyaktena bhuñjīthā mā gṛdhaḥ kasya svid dhanam

"Everything animate or inanimate that is within the universe is controlled and owned by the Lord. One should therefore accept only those things necessary for himself, which are set aside as his quota, and one should not accept other things, knowing well to whom they belong."

Here the *Īśopaniṣad* says that everything belongs to God. Then how can you claim, "This is our American land" or "This is our Indian land"? This is illusion: what is not yours, you are claiming to be yours. Even your body is not yours. Nature has given you your body according to your karma, but ultimately your body belongs to Kṛṣṇa. Suppose I rent a house. It is not my house; it is the landlord's. This is a fact. But if I move into the house and then claim, "This is my house," I will get into trouble. Similarly, everything we are using for our comfort and livelihood has been given to us by God. The body is given by God, and the maintenance for the body is also given by God. You maintain your body by eating fruits, grains, milk, or even meat. But who is supplying these things? You cannot create them in your factories. The *Vedas* say, *eko bahūnāṁ vidadhāti kāmān:* "The Lord is supplying everyone's necessities." Understanding that everything belongs to God is Kṛṣṇa consciousness.

Now we have so many ignoble things in our hearts, such as falsely claiming God's property as our own. But Kṛṣṇa is within our hearts, and when He sees that we are regularly and seriously hearing *kṛṣṇa-kathā,* He will wash off all these ignoble things: *hṛdy antaḥ-stho hy abhadrāṇi vidhunoti*. So by providing an opportunity for everyone to hear the *Śrīmad-Bhāgavatam, Bhagavad-gītā,* and other sources of *kṛṣṇa-kathā,* the Kṛṣṇa consciousness movement is helping human society become purified and thus live in peace, happiness, and prosperity.

13

Escaping the Clutches of Harmful Desires

naṣṭa-prāyeṣv abhadreṣu
nityaṁ bhāgavata-sevayā
bhagavaty uttama-śloke
bhaktir bhavati naiṣṭhikī

By regular attendance in classes on the Bhāgavatam and by rendering of service to the pure devotee, all that is troublesome to the heart is almost completely destroyed, and loving service unto the Personality of Godhead, who is praised with transcendental songs, is established as an irrevocable fact.

Śrīmad-Bhāgavatam 1.2.18

Here is the remedy for eliminating all inauspicious things within the heart, which are considered to be obstacles in the path of self-realization. The remedy is the association of the *Bhāgavatas*. There are two types of *Bhāgavatas,* namely the book *Bhāgavata* and the devotee *Bhāgavata*. Both the *Bhāgavatas* are competent remedies, and both of them or either of them can be good enough to eliminate the obstacles. A devotee *Bhāgavata* is as good as the book *Bhāgavata* because the devotee *Bhāgavata* leads his life in terms of the book *Bhāgavata* and the book *Bhāgavata* is full of information about the Personality of Godhead and His pure devotees, who are also *Bhāgavatas*. *Bhāgavata* book and person are identical.

The devotee *Bhāgavata* is a direct representative of Bhagavān, the Personality of Godhead. So by pleasing the devotee *Bhāgavata* one can receive the benefit of the book *Bhāgavata*. Human reason fails to understand how by serving the devotee *Bhāgavata* or the book *Bhāgavata* one gets gradual promotion on the path of devotion. But actually these are facts explained by Śrīla Nāradadeva, who happened to be a maidservant's son in his previous life. The maidservant was engaged in the menial service of some sages, and thus he also came into contact with them. And simply by associating with them and accepting the remnants of food left by the sages, the son of the maidservant got the chance to become the great devotee and personality Śrīla Nāradadeva. These are the miraculous effects of the association of *Bhāgavatas*. And to understand these effects practically, it should be noted that by such sincere association of the *Bhāgavatas* one is sure to receive transcendental knowledge very easily, with the result that one becomes fixed in the devotional service of the Lord. The more progress is made in devotional service under the guidance of the *Bhāgavatas,* the more one becomes fixed in the transcendental loving service of the Lord. The messages of the book *Bhāgavata,* therefore, have to be received from the devotee *Bhāgavata,* and the combination of these two *Bhāgavatas* will help the neophyte devotee to make progress on and on.

Generally, people do not understand the need for making spiritual progress and cleansing the heart of all dirty things (*abhadrāṇi*). Material life means dirty life, uncivilized life, yet people think that having nice clothes and a nice apartment and a nicely washed body means they are civilized. They do not know how the contamination within their hearts has attacked them.

In the name of civilization, people have created so many unnecessary things, called *anarthas*. For example, thousands of years ago, in the Vedic age, when there was no so-called advancement of civilization, people used to eat from utensils made of silver or gold, or at least some kind of metal. Now people are using plastic, yet they are still proud of their advanced civilization. Actually, the plastic utensils are unnecessary. Another example: two hundred years ago in India there was no industry, but people were so happy. They did not have to travel two hundred miles or five hundred miles away from home to earn their livelihood. In Europe and America I have seen that some people are daily flying by airplane to the place where they earn their livelihood. From Toronto they are flying to Montreal—almost five hundred miles. Nearly everyone has to travel at least fifty miles. In New York many people come from a distant place on Long Island, cross the river, and then take a bus to reach their place of employment. All this travel is simply unnecessary.

Cāṇakya Paṇḍita asks, "Who is happy?" He answers, "The man who does not work away from home and who is not a debtor—he is happy." Very simple. Yet now we see that practically everyone works away from home and everyone is a great debtor. So how can they be happy? In America the banks canvass, "Borrow money from us, purchase a motorcar, purchase a house, and as soon as you get your salary, give it to us." Or they offer, "Take this bank card." It should be known as a bank*rupt* card. If you take the card and deposit your money in the bank, then you can purchase whatever you like with the card. But soon you are without any money, and all you have left is that card.

So, all these *anarthas* can immediately be finished if you take up the process of Kṛṣṇa consciousness, or *bhakti-yoga: anarthopaśamaṁ sākṣād bhakti-yogam adhokṣaje*. A good example is our students in the Kṛṣṇa consciousness movement. Many are from America or Europe, and they knew very well how to increase *anarthas*. But as soon as they joined our Society they no longer had to pay the cinema bill, the gambling bill, and so many other bills. Even the medical bills were decreased almost to nil. Does a person die without smoking? No. It is an *anartha*. One becomes habituated to smoking due to bad association: *saṅgāt sañjāyate kāmaḥ*. Because of bad association one learns how to smoke, how to gamble, how to eat meat, and how to take intoxicants. In America the government is spending millions of dollars to stop this intoxication habit among the young people. But the government does not know how to stop it. Here is the remedy: Kṛṣṇa consciousness. It is practical. Anyone who seriously takes up the process of Kṛṣṇa consciousness can immediately give up all bad habits, including intoxication. But still the government will not patronize the Kṛṣṇa consciousness movement. They'd rather spend lavishly on some useless program.

Because the modern people do not know how to get out of the clutches of all these unnecessary things, the learned Śrīla Vyāsadeva wrote the *Śrīmad-Bhāgavatam: lokasyājānato vidvāṁś cakre sātvata-saṁhitām.* Take shelter of the *Śrīmad-Bhāgavatam* and you will perfectly learn how to diminish your unnecessary things. The simple process is given in the previous verse (*Bhāg.* 1.2.17):

śṛṇvatāṁ sva-kathāḥ kṛṣṇaḥ puṇya-śravaṇa-kīrtanaḥ
hṛdy antaḥ-stho hy abhadrāṇi vidhunoti suhṛt satām

If you simply hear about Kṛṣṇa from the *Śrīmad-Bhāgavatam* or the *Bhagavad-gītā,* Kṛṣṇa Himself will cleanse away your *anarthas.* In the *Bhagavad-gītā* Kṛṣṇa is directly speaking about Himself. But don't misinterpret His words. Simply hear them as Arjuna did. Someone may say, "Arjuna heard the *Bhagavad-gītā* directly from Kṛṣṇa, but now Kṛṣṇa is absent. So how can we hear it as Arjuna did?" Because Kṛṣṇa is absolute, He is nondifferent from His words. So if you read the *Bhagavad-gītā* as it is, receiving it through disciplic succession, then your reading is as good as Arjuna's hearing directly from Kṛṣṇa. But if you give your own interpretation of the *Bhagavad-gītā,* or hear the interpretation of a nondevotee, you'll remain a rascal.

Sanātana Gosvāmī has forbidden us to hear about Kṛṣṇa from nondevotees:

avaiṣṇava-mukhodgīrṇaṁ pūtaṁ hari-kathāmṛtam
śravaṇaṁ naiva kartavyaṁ sarpocchiṣṭaṁ yathā payaḥ

"One should not hear anything about Kṛṣṇa from a non-Vaiṣṇava. Milk touched by the lips of a serpent has poisonous effects; similarly, talks about Kṛṣṇa given by a non-Vaiṣṇava are also poisonous." Sometimes, in India, people who do not follow the principles of Vaiṣṇava behavior become professional reciters of the *Śrīmad-Bhāgavatam* and hold seven-day public readings, called *bhāgavata-saptāha.* Such hearing of the *Śrīmad-Bhāgavatam* is forbidden. The present verse recommends *nityaṁ bhāgavata-sevayā,* "regular hearing of the *Bhāgavatam,*" not *saptāhaṁ bhāgavata-sevayā,* "one-week's hearing of the *Bhāgavatam.*" Is the *Bhāgavatam* such a thing that you can understand everything just by hearing it for one week? You will not understand one *word* by reading the *Bhāgavatam* for only a week, what to speak of all eighteen thousand verses. The whole of Vedic knowledge is contained in the *Bhāgavatam* (*nigama-kalpa-taror galitaṁ phalam*), so what will you understand by only a week's reading?

The real prescription is given here: *nityaṁ bhāgavata-sevayā.* Every day you should hear the *Bhāgavatam,* and at every moment you should remember the *Bhāgavatam.* Then *naṣṭa-prāyeṣv abhadreṣu:* the dirty things in your heart will be eradicated. This is the essence of the Kṛṣṇa consciousness movement—to provide you with an opportunity to hear about Kṛṣṇa patiently so that the dirty things within your heart will be cleansed away. What those dirty things are will be mentioned in the next verse.

14

Bhakti-Yoga: The Quickest Way To Peace and Bliss

. . . . . .

tadā rajas-tamo-bhāvāḥ
kāma-lobhādayaś ca ye
ceta etair anāviddhaṁ
sthitaṁ sattve prasīdati

As soon as irrevocable loving service is established in the heart, the effects of nature's modes of passion and ignorance, such as lust, desire, and hankering, disappear from the heart. Then the devotee is established in goodness, and he becomes completely happy.

Śrīmad-Bhāgavatam 1.2.19

A living being in his normal constitutional position is fully satisfied in spiritual bliss. This state of existence is called *brahma-bhūta* or *ātmānandī,* or the state of self-satisfaction. This self-satisfaction is not like the satisfaction of the inactive fool. The inactive fool is in the state of foolish ignorance, whereas the self-satisfied *ātmānandī* is transcendental to the material state of existence. This stage of perfection is attained as soon as one is fixed in irrevocable devotional service. Devotional service is not inactivity, but the unalloyed activity of the soul.

The soul's activity becomes adulterated in contact with matter, and as such the diseased activities are expressed in the form of lust, desire, hankering, inactivity, foolishness, and sleep. The effect of devotional service becomes manifest by complete elimination of these effects of passion and ignorance. The devotee is fixed at once in the mode of goodness, and he makes further progress to rise to the position of *vasudeva,* or the state of unmixed *sattva,* or *śuddha-sattva*. Only in this *śuddha-sattva* state can one always see Kṛṣṇa eye to eye by dint of pure affection for the Lord.

A devotee is always in the mode of unalloyed goodness; therefore he harms no one. But the nondevotee, however educated he may be, is always harmful. A devotee is neither foolish nor passionate. The harmful, foolish, and passionate cannot be devotees of the Lord, however they may advertise themselves as devotees by outward dress. A devotee is always qualified with all the good qualities of God. Quantitatively such qualifications may be different, but qualitatively the Lord and His devotee are one and the same.

The nondevotees, on the other hand, act under the influence of a combination of the three modes of material nature—the mode of goodness, the mode of passion, and the mode of ignorance. These modes combine in unlimited ways to produce unlimited varieties of people. Progressive life begins when one endeavors to come to the platform of the mode of goodness. By undergoing training one can come to this platform, just as by undergoing training an illiterate, uncultured, animallike man can become civilized. Even cats and dogs and tigers can be trained to be obedient. That is our practical experience.

There are two kinds of training processes for elevating the human being to the stage of pure goodness. One is the scheduled, step-by-step process: *tapasā brahmacaryeṇa śamena ca damena ca.* In this process one undergoes various austerities (*tapasya*), controls the sex impulse by practicing celibacy (*brahmacarya*), and in general controls the senses and the mind (*śama dama*). Also, one may give wealth in charity (*tyāga*). This is the gradual process of elevation.

But there is another process—Kṛṣṇa consciousness, or *bhakti-yoga*. Suppose you have to go up to the top floor of a ten-story building. You can go step by step, or you can take the elevator. *Bhakti-yoga* is the elevator. If you take up this process, then you will very quickly reach the top floor. Otherwise, you have to go step by step by step. Although both processes lead to the topmost floor, one is very slow and the other very quick.

The beginning of *bhakti-yoga* is hearing about Kṛṣṇa. As described in the present verses of the *Bhāgavatam,* the result of hearing about Kṛṣṇa regularly is that the dirty things in the heart are cleansed almost to nil (*naṣṭa-prāyeṣv abhadreṣu*); then one becomes steady in devotional service, surpasses the modes of passion and ignorance, and is promoted to the platform of goodness (*sthitaṁ sattve prasīdati*). And as soon as you come to the platform of goodness, you are freed from lust and greed, the effects of the lower modes of passion and ignorance.

The whole world is moving due to the impulse of lust and greed. Those who are influenced by the lower qualities of material nature are never satisfied: "Give me more, give me more, give me more." But no matter how much one gets, one is not satisfied. A man will think, "If I can just increase my income to one thousand dollars a month, I will be satisfied." But as soon as he gets one thousand dollars, he wants a hundred thousand. Even the millionaires are not satisfied. In Paris I have seen lusty old men going to clubs. They enter the club by paying fifty dollars, and there they find young women and wine—that is their pleasure. On the one side they are not satisfied even with millions of dollars, and on the other side they want to enjoy young women. Simply greedy and lusty, that's all.

So, to become Kṛṣṇa conscious means to become free from lust and greed: *ceta etair anāviddham. Viddham* means "piercing." Lust and greed are always piercing and pinching the heart: "Come on, come on, enjoy!" But when you are actually a little advanced in Kṛṣṇa consciousness, these things will no longer pinch you because your heart will be cleansed. Then you will always be joyful. As Kṛṣṇa says in the *Bhagavad-gītā* (18.54),

> *brahma-bhūtaḥ prasannātmā na śocati na kāṅkṣati*
> *samaḥ sarveṣu bhūteṣu mad-bhaktiṁ labhate parām*

When you come to the *brahma-bhūta* stage, the platform of liberation, you become fully joyful and no longer lament or hanker over material things (*na śocati na kāṅkṣati*). In material consciousness we hanker after something we do not possess, and we lament when we lose something. But in Kṛṣṇa consciousness we are free from these effects of the modes of passion and ignorance. In such consciousness you will be able to see everyone on the spiritual platform. As Kṛṣṇa explains earlier in the *Bhagavad-gītā* (5.18),

vidyā-vinaya-sampanne brāhmaṇe gavi hastini
śuni caiva śva-pāke ca paṇḍitāḥ sama-darśinaḥ

One in Kṛṣṇa consciousness is truly learned, and thus he sees cats and dogs and human beings equally. He doesn't see the outward dress of the body but sees the spirit soul. "Here is a spirit soul," he thinks "part and parcel of Kṛṣṇa." That kind of vision is the basis of universal brotherhood. Brotherhood will not come by passing resolutions in the United Nations. That is not possible. You have to come to the spiritual platform; then there will be love, brotherhood, equality, and fraternity. Otherwise it is all bogus propaganda.

Finally, one who comes to the spiritual platform—the *brahma-bhūta* stage—attains pure devotional service to Kṛṣṇa (*mad-bhaktiṁ labhate parām*). In other words, one becomes completely fit to serve Kṛṣṇa, and Kṛṣṇa accepts your service at that time. This stage is further described in the next verse.

15

Bhakti-Yoga Is Science, Not Sentiment

evaṁ prasanna-manaso
bhagavad-bhakti-yogataḥ
bhagavat-tattva-vijñānaṁ
mukta-saṅgasya jāyate

Thus established in the mode of unalloyed goodness, the man whose mind has been enlivened by contact with devotional service to the Lord gains positive scientific knowledge of the Personality of Godhead in the stage of liberation from all material association.

Śrīmad-Bhāgavatam 1.2.20

In the *Bhagavad-gītā* (7.3) it is said that out of many thousands of ordinary men, one fortunate man endeavors for perfection in life. Mostly men are conducted by the modes of passion and ignorance, and thus they are engaged always in lust, desire, hankerings, ignorance, and sleep. Out of many such manlike animals, there is actually a man who knows the responsibility of human life and thus tries to make life perfect by following the prescribed duties. And out of many thousands of such persons who have thus attained success in human life, one may know scientifically about the Personality of Godhead Śrī Kṛṣṇa. In the same *Bhagavad-gītā* (18.55) it is also said that scientific knowledge of Śrī Kṛṣṇa is understood only by the process of devotional service (*bhakti-yoga*).

The very same thing is confirmed herein in the above words. No ordinary man, or even one who has attained success in human life, can know scientifically or perfectly the Personality of Godhead. Perfection of human life is attained when one can understand that he is not the product of matter but is in fact spirit. And as soon as one understands that he has nothing to do with matter, he at once ceases his material hankerings and becomes enlivened as a spiritual being. This attainment of success is possible when one is above the modes of passion and ignorance, or, in other words, when one is actually a *brāhmaṇa* by qualification.

A *brāhmaṇa* is the symbol of *sattva-guṇa,* or the mode of goodness. And others, who are not in the mode of goodness, are either *kṣatriyas, vaiśyas, śūdras,* or less than *śūdras*. The brahminical stage is the highest stage of human life because of its good qualities. So one cannot be a devotee unless one at least qualifies as a *brāhmaṇa*. The devotee is already a *brāhmaṇa* by action. But that is not the end of it. As referred to above, such a *brāhmaṇa* has to become a Vaiṣṇava in fact to be actually in the transcendental stage. A pure Vaiṣṇava is a liberated soul and is transcendental even to the position of a *brāhmaṇa*. In the material stage even a *brāhmaṇa* is also a conditioned soul because although in the brahminical stage the conception of Brahman or transcendence is realized, scientific knowledge of the Supreme Lord is lacking. One has to surpass the brahminical stage and reach the *vasudeva* stage to understand the Personality of Godhead, Kṛṣṇa.

The science of the Personality of Godhead is the subject matter for study by the postgraduate students in the spiritual line. Foolish men, or men with a poor fund of knowledge, do not understand the Supreme Lord, and they interpret Kṛṣṇa according to their respective whims. The fact is, however, that one cannot understand the science of the Personality of Godhead unless one is freed from the contamination of the material modes, even up to the stage of a *brāhmaṇa*. When a qualified *brāhmaṇa* factually becomes a Vaiṣṇava, in the enlivened state of liberation he can know what is actually the Personality of Godhead.

The process of *bhakti-yoga* is not a concoction or speculation. It is a science. As stated in the present verse, *bhagavat-tattva-vijñānam:* "one gains scientific knowledge of the Personality of Godhead." *Vijñāna* means "science." In mathematics, "Two plus two equals four" is always true. You cannot make it equal five according to your whims. No. Because mathematics is a science, whether you are in America or India or England, you will find that everyone accepts that two plus two equals four. Similarly, you cannot imagine God according to your whims. Nowadays many people say, "You can imagine your God, and I can imagine my God." No, there is no question of imagining anything about God. As stated here, the scientific truth of God can be understood by a person who is *mukta-saṅga,* freed from material association. Such a person, being transcendental to the lower modes of nature, is jubilant and enlightened (*prasanna-manasaḥ*). As long as you are under the jurisdiction of the modes of ignorance and passion, there is no question of jubilation or enlightenment. Therefore you have to come to the platform of pure goodness.

The previous verse stated, *ceta etair anāviddhaṁ sthitaṁ sattve prasīdati:* "When the heart is free of passion and ignorance and fixed in goodness, one becomes jubilant." At that time one can understand how foolish it is for people to work so hard like cats and dogs simply for material benefits. Human life is meant for understanding God (*athāto brahma-jijñāsā*). The foolish animals cannot understand God, but human beings can because of their developed consciousness.

However, to take advantage of this developed consciousness you must rise to the platform of goodness. Then, by studying nature, you will see that one does not have to work so hard for getting the material necessities. The birds and beasts are getting their food, they are getting their mates, they are being protected in their own way, they have some nest or hole to sleep in. Even the ants are being provided for. When we sit down in a garden we see that even the ant has its family, its home, its food—everything is there. From the ant to the elephant, all are getting their necessities of life. Who is supplying?

So, one who is in the mode of goodness will ask, "Since God is supplying life's necessities to all 8,400,000 species of life, why are the so-called civilized human beings struggling so hard for these things?" We have greater intelligence than the animals; therefore our struggle for existence should be less than theirs. Still, it is greater. What sort of civilization is this? This is not civilization. Everyone wants a peaceful, calm life, but instead the modern human society forces everyone to work like an ass the whole day and night simply to satisfy the four basic necessities of life—eating, sleeping, mating, and defending. And even then these are not guaranteed. When I lived in India before going to America, I thought that since America is very rich the people there have no problem eating, sleeping, and so on. But the Americans have created a civilization where a certain section of the people are obliged to lie down on the street or in a park, and they have no proper dress, not enough food, and no fixed-up sex life. In such a so-called civilization, people are always disturbed and full of anxiety. Then how can they understand God?

To understand God you first have to come to the stage of tranquillity. Then, when one understands God, one will be *prasanna-manasa,* always jubilant. One can become jubilant only by practicing *bhakti-yoga,* not by any other process. There are many other yoga systems—*karma-yoga, jñāna-yoga, dhyāna-yoga, haṭha-yoga.* Every endeavor for spiritual enlightenment is a type of yoga. But real yoga is *bhagavad-bhakti-yoga,* devotional service to the Supreme Lord. Therefore in the *Bhagavad-gītā* (6.47) Kṛṣṇa says,

> *yogināṁ api sarveṣāṁ mad-gatenāntar-ātmanā*
> *śraddhāvān bhajate yo māṁ sa me yuktatamo mataḥ*

"Of all yogis, the one with great faith who always abides in Me, thinks of Me within himself, and renders transcendental loving service to Me—he is the most intimately united with Me in yoga and is the highest of all. That is My opinion." So the first-class yogi is the devotee who is always thinking of Kṛṣṇa within his heart by chanting the Hare Kṛṣṇa *mantra*—Hare Kṛṣṇa, Hare Kṛṣṇa, Kṛṣṇa Kṛṣṇa, Hare Hare/ Hare Rāma, Hare Rāma, Rāma Rāma, Hare Hare. That is *bhagavad-bhakti-yoga.* And if the devotee progresses nicely, following all the rules and regulations, then one day he will understand God in truth and become *prasanna-manasa*—enlightened, engladdened, and free of all lamentation and hankering.

God is not so cheap. "Come on," say the cheaters, "I shall show you God. You haven't got to follow any rules and regulations." People who want God cheaply are prone to be cheated, and there are many cheaters who will take advantage of them. The actual process of understanding God is a science. Suppose someone says, "I shall teach you the science of chemistry within a second. Give me some money." Or "I shall teach you mathematics within a second. Give me some money." Will you agree to such impossible proposals? Then why are these rascals allowed to mislead people into believing they can understand God so cheaply? *Bhakti-yoga* is science, not sentiment.

Rūpa Gosvāmī instructs us,

> *śruti-smṛti-purāṇādi-pañcarātra-vidhiṁ vinā*
> *aikāntikī harer bhaktir utpātāyaiva kalpate*

So many rascals are causing a disturbance in society by posing that they have understood God without reference to the Vedic literature, the revealed scriptures. These include the *śruti,* such as the four *Vedas* and the *Upaniṣads*, the *smṛti,* such as the *Bhagavad-gītā,* the *Purāṇas,* such as the *Śrīmad-Bhāgavatam,* and the *pañcarātras,* such as the *Nārada-pañcarātra*. To understand God is a great science. How can you ignore the authorized books of knowledge and manufacture a process for knowing God?

Therefore any religion without a scientific, philosophical understanding of God is simply sentiment. It is not religion.

And philosophy without religion is simply mental speculation. In other words, that philosophy which does not answer the ultimate questions—What is the Absolute Truth? What is God?—is useless. Religion and philosophy should be combined so that we can scientifically understand who is God, what is our relationship with God, what is our duty toward God, and so on.

From its beginning the *Śrīmad-Bhāgavatam* kicks out all cheating so-called religions and presents *bhagavat-tattva-vijñāna,* the genuine science of God. This science has to be studied, it has to be practiced, and it has to be realized. We are presenting this scientific understanding as Kṛṣṇa consciousness. It is not for the sentimentalists but for those who are serious about perfecting their lives.

It is not so easy to reach perfection and understand Śrī Kṛṣṇa. As Kṛṣṇa states in the *Bhagavad-gītā* (4.3),

manuṣyāṇāṁ sahasreṣu kaścid yatati siddhaye
yatatām api siddhānāṁ kaścin māṁ vetti tattvataḥ

"Out of many thousands of men, one may endeavor for perfection, and of those who have achieved perfection, hardly one knows Me in truth." Still, because Kṛṣṇa is compassionate upon the fallen souls of this age, He appeared as Lord Caitanya and freely distributed Himself. That is His prerogative. If Kṛṣṇa wants to distribute Himself freely, that is His right, and then the whole process becomes very easy. Otherwise, it is not so easy to understand Kṛṣṇa. For example, to earn a million dollars is not so easy, but if you are fortunate and meet someone who freely gives you a million dollars, that is a different thing.

Therefore Rūpa Gosvāmī glorified Lord Caitanya as the most munificent incarnation: "I offer my respectful obeisances unto the Supreme Lord Śrī Kṛṣṇa Caitanya, who is more magnanimous than any other avatar, even Kṛṣṇa Himself, because He is bestowing freely what no one else has ever given—pure love of Kṛṣṇa." If we follow in the footsteps of Rūpa Gosvāmī, we can understand Lord Caitanya. And if we get the favor of Lord Caitanya, we can very easily understand Kṛṣṇa.

16

When the Kṛṣṇa Sun Rises in the Heart

bhidyate hṛdaya-granthiś
chidyante sarva-saṁśayāḥ
kṣīyante cāsya karmāṇi
dṛṣṭa evātmanīśvare

Thus the knot in the heart is pierced, and all misgivings are cut to pieces. The chain of fruitive actions is terminated when one sees the Self as master.

Śrīmad-Bhāgavatam 1.2.21

Attaining scientific knowledge of the Personality of Godhead means seeing one's own self simultaneously. As far as the identity of the living being as spirit self is concerned, there are a number of speculations and misgivings. The materialist does not believe in the existence of the spirit self, and empiric philosophers believe in the impersonal feature of the whole spirit without individuality of the living beings. But the transcendentalists affirm that the soul and the Supersoul are two different identities, qualitatively one but quantitatively different. There are many other theories, but all these different speculations are at once cleared off as soon as Śrī Kṛṣṇa is realized in truth by the process of *bhakti-yoga*. Śrī Kṛṣṇa is like the sun, and the materialistic speculations about the Absolute Truth are like the darkest midnight. As soon as the Kṛṣṇa sun is arisen within one's heart, the darkness of materialistic speculations about the Absolute Truth and the living beings is at once cleared off. In the presence of the sun, the darkness cannot stand, and the relative truths that were hidden within the dense darkness of ignorance become clearly manifested by the mercy of Kṛṣṇa, who is residing in everyone's heart as the Supersoul.

In the *Bhagavad-gītā* (10.11) the Lord says that in order to show special favor to His pure devotees He personally eradicates the dense darkness of all misgivings by switching on the light of pure knowledge within the heart of a devotee. Therefore, because of the Personality of Godhead's taking charge of illuminating the heart of His devotee, certainly a devotee, engaged in His service in transcendental love, cannot remain in darkness. He comes to know everything of the absolute and the relative truths. The devotee cannot remain in darkness, and because a devotee is enlightened by the Personality of Godhead, his knowledge is certainly perfect. This is not the case for those who speculate on the Absolute Truth by dint of their own limited power of approach. Perfect knowledge is called *paramparā,* or deductive knowledge coming down from the authority to the submissive aural receiver who is bona fide by service and surrender. One cannot challenge the authority of the Supreme and know Him also at the same time. He reserves the right of not being exposed to such a challenging spirit of an insignificant spark of the whole, a spark subjected to the control of illusory energy. The devotees are submissive, and therefore the transcendental knowledge descends from the Personality of Godhead to Brahmā and from Brahmā to his sons and disciples in succession. This process is helped by the Supersoul within such devotees. That is the perfect way of learning transcendental knowledge.

This enlightenment perfectly enables the devotee to distinguish spirit from matter because the knot of spirit and matter is untied by the Lord. This knot is called *ahaṅkāra,* and it falsely obliges a living being to become identified with matter. As soon as this knot is loosened, therefore, all the clouds of doubt are at once cleared off. One sees his master and fully engages himself in the transcendental loving service of the Lord, making a full termination of the chain of fruitive action. In material existence, a living being creates his own chain of fruitive work and enjoys the good and bad effects of those actions life after life. But as soon as he engages himself in the loving service of the Lord, he at once becomes free from the chain of karma. His actions no longer create any reaction.

This is the stage of complete liberation. In the previous verse it was said, *bhagavat-tattva-vijñānaṁ mukta-saṅgasya jāyate.* This means that the science of God, or the science of the Absolute Truth, becomes manifest to the liberated soul. Sometimes we find that someone poses as a great devotee very much advanced in spiritual understanding, but he cannot even give up smoking cigarettes. That means he's not liberated. For one who actually has a taste for spiritual life, all material attachments diminish to nil. This is the sign that one is actually liberated.

The first statement in the present verse is *bhidyate hṛdaya-granthiḥ,* "factual understanding of God cuts the knots in the heart." Material life begins with the strong knot in the heart called sex desire. A man hankers for a woman and a woman hankers for a man, and their mutual attachment begins their material life. Not only in human society but also in animal society, bird society, insect society, you'll find this sex attachment. This is the primary *hṛdaya-granthiḥ,* knot in the heart.

Therefore in the Vedic civilization the first lesson a student learns is *brahmacarya,* celibacy. Abstaining from sex is not such an easy thing: it requires *tapasya,* training in austerity. One has to practice how to control the mind and the senses. At present, far from being taught to practice *tapasya,* the university students are given all kinds of luxuries. Especially in the Western countries, the boys and girls are educated together, and they even live in the same building. So there is no question of *brahmacarya.* Rather, the hard knot of sex desire binds their hearts more and more.

So, to cut the knot of sex desire and other knots binding the heart, one must follow two parallel lines: On one side a person should cultivate Kṛṣṇa consciousness, and on the other he should try to give up all his bad habits. Both sides must be there if he wants to advance. For example, when a person is diseased the doctor prescribes some medicine, and at the same time he instructs the patient in what to eat and what not to eat. That is the proper way of treatment. It is not that the patient can eat whatever he likes and if he simply takes the medicine he will be cured. Similarly, it is nonsense to think that you can do whatever you like and if you simply chant Hare Kṛṣṇa you will become spiritually advanced. You have to practice *tapasya* by voluntarily accepting a little inconvenience. For instance, we have instructed that everyone in our Kṛṣṇa consciousness society must give up illicit sex, meat-eating, intoxication, and gambling. In addition, all our students must rise early in the morning (before four), take a bath, attend *maṅgala-ārati,* and study the scriptures. These are all austerities, in which we voluntarily give up things we may like and accept things we may not like. Of course, if a person takes to Kṛṣṇa consciousness seriously, Kṛṣṇa helps him become qualified in all these matters.

The next statement in the present verse is *chidyante sarva-saṁśayāḥ,* "all doubts are cut to pieces." One who is not advanced in Kṛṣṇa consciousness has so many doubts. He may even doubt that he is the soul, not the body. But as soon as he becomes fully conversant in the science of God (*bhagavat-tattva-vijñānam*), all his doubts are wiped away and he knows with certainty, "I am a spirit soul, an eternal servant of Kṛṣṇa."

Next the *Bhāgavatam* says, *kṣīyante cāsya karmāṇi:* "the chain of fruitive action and reaction is terminated." We are bound up in this material existence due to our karma, fruitive actions. According to your past karma you have your present body, and you are preparing your next body by how you are acting now. All human beings have certain common factors—two hands, two legs, one head—but each body is different because everyone's karma is different. So, we have to stop this karma. How? Kṛṣṇa explains in the *Bhagavad-gītā* (3.9),

yajñārthāt karmaṇo 'nyatra loko 'yaṁ karma-bandhanaḥ
tad-arthaṁ karma kaunteya mukta-saṅgaḥ samācara

If you simply work for Kṛṣṇa, then you will not be bound up by karma. Otherwise, whether your activities are good or bad by ordinary calculation, you will be bound up by the karmic reactions.

So, one who is fixed in devotional service to Kṛṣṇa is actually liberated from all material bondage. But as soon as you deviate from devotional service, Kṛṣṇa's illusory energy (*māyā*) will immediately capture you. Śrī Caitanya Mahāprabhu gives the perfect analogy in the *Caitanya-caritāmṛta* (*Madhya* 22.31): "Kṛṣṇa is just like the sunshine, and *māyā* is just like darkness. Wherever the sun shines, there is no possibility of darkness." So keep yourself always in Kṛṣṇa consciousness. Then there will be no possibility of *māyā,* which forces us to engage in fruitive activities (karma).

Concerning the eradication of karma through devotional service, the *Brahma-saṁhitā* (5.54) says,

yas tv indragopam athavendram aho sva-karma-
bandhānurūpa-phala-bhājanam ātanoti
karmāṇi nirdahati kintu ca bhakti-bhājāṁ
govindam ādi-puruṣaṁ tam ahaṁ bhajāmi

"From Lord Indra, the King of heaven, down to the small insect known as the *indra-gopa,* everyone is enjoying or suffering the results of his karma. But a devotee's karmic reactions are burned up by the Lord Himself."

You can be promoted to the post of Indra, the King of heaven, provided you have performed sufficient pious activities, just as you can become a high court judge if you have sufficient education. All the great demigods—Indra, Candra, Sūrya, Brahmā—have achieved their posts on account of their great pious activities, called *puṇya-karma*. Similarly, the hogs, dogs, and other animals are suffering in their respective bodies due to *pāpa-karma,* impious activities. So, everyone is suffering or enjoying the reactions of his karma and in this way remaining bound up in this material world. It is very easy to understand. But, *karmāṇi nirdahati kintu ca bhakti-bhājām:* the karma of those who have taken to Kṛṣṇa consciousness in devotional service is burned up. In other words, for the devotees of Kṛṣṇa there are no karmic reactions. If you sow a chickpea in the ground, it will grow into a plant, but if you fry a chickpea and then sow it in the ground, it will not grow. So we should fry our karma by devotional service. Then our activities will not produce any karmic reaction.

Unless you have completely eradicated your karmic reactions, you cannot be promoted to the spiritual world. In other words, as long as you continue to perform fruitive activities, you'll have to accept some type of material body, birth after birth. Therefore Lord Ṛṣabhadeva says in the Fifth Canto of the *Śrīmad-Bhāgavatam* (5.5.4),

nūnaṁ pramattaḥ kurute vikarma
yad indriya-prītaya āpṛṇoti
na sādhu manye yata ātmano 'yam
asann api kleśada āsa dehaḥ

"Those without knowledge of the spirit soul are mad after materialistic activities, and they perform all kinds of sinful activities simply for sense gratification. Such activities are inauspicious because they force one to accept an abominable body in the next life."

For a devotee, however, there is no more karma, and so there is no more material body. Kṛṣṇa confirms this in the *Bhagavad-gītā* (4.9): *tyaktvā dehaṁ punar janma naiti mām eti.* After giving up his present body, a devotee does not get another material body, but rather in his spiritual body he goes back home, back to Godhead.

The same idea is expressed in the present verse of the *Bhāgavatam: kṣīyante cāsya karmāṇi dṛṣṭa evātmanīśvare.* Freed of all karmic reactions, the devotee fully realizes his relationship with God, thinking "I am an eternal servant of God, or Kṛṣṇa." And because he realizes his actual identity, he always engages in pure devotional service. That is the perfection of life.

APPENDIXES

About the Author

His Divine Grace A. C. Bhaktivedanta Swami Prabhupāda appeared in this world in 1896 in Calcutta, India. He first met his spiritual master, Śrīla Bhaktisiddhānta Sarasvatī Gosvāmī, in Calcutta in 1922. Bhaktisiddhānta Sarasvatī, a prominent religious scholar and the founder of sixty-four Gauḍīya Maṭhas (Vedic institutes), liked this educated young man and convinced him to dedicate his life to teaching Vedic knowledge. Śrīla Prabhupāda became his student and, in 1932, his formally initiated disciple.

At their first meeting, in 1922, Bhaktisiddhānta Sarasvatī asked Śrīla Prabhupāda to broadcast Vedic knowledge in English. In the years that followed, Śrīla Prabhupāda wrote a commentary on the *Bhagavad-gītā,* assisted the Gauḍīya Maṭha in its work, and, in 1944, started *Back to Godhead,* an English fortnightly magazine. Single-handedly, Śrīla Prabhupāda edited it, typed the manuscripts, checked the galley proofs, and even distributed the individual copies. The magazine is now being continued by his disciples in the West.

In 1950 Śrīla Prabhupāda retired from married life, adopting the *vānaprastha* (retired) order to devote more time to his studies and writing. He traveled to the holy city of Vṛndāvana, where he lived in humble circumstances in the historic temple of Rādhā-Dāmodara. There he engaged for several years in deep study and writing. He accepted the renounced order of life (*sannyāsa*) in 1959. At Rādhā-Dāmodara, Śrīla Prabhupāda began work on his life's masterpiece: a multivolume commentated translation of the 18,000-verse *Śrīmad-Bhāgavatam* (*Bhāgavata Purāṇa*). He also wrote *Easy Journey to Other Planets.*

After publishing three volumes of the *Bhāgavatam,* Śrīla Prabhupāda came to the United States, in September 1965, to fulfill the mission of his spiritual master. Subsequently, His Divine Grace wrote more than fifty volumes of authoritative commentated translations and summary studies of the philosophical and religious classics of India.

When he first arrived in New York City, Śrīla Prabhupāda was nearly penniless. Only after a year of great difficulty did he establish the International Society for Krishna Consciousness, in July of 1966. Before he passed away on November 14, 1977, he had guided the Society and seen it grow to a worldwide confederation of more than one hundred *āśramas,* schools, temples, institutes, and farm communities.

In 1972 His Divine Grace introduced the Vedic system of primary and secondary education in the West by founding the *gurukula* school in Dallas, Texas. Since then his disciples have established similar schools throughout the United States and the rest of the world.

Śrīla Prabhupāda also inspired the construction of several large international cultural centers in India. The center at Śrīdhāma Māyāpur is the site for a planned spiritual city, an ambitious project for which construction will extend over many years to come. In Vṛndāvana are the magnificent Kṛṣṇa-Balarāma Temple and International Guesthouse, *gurukula* school, and Śrīla Prabhupāda Memorial and Museum. There are also major cultural and educational centers in Mumbai, New Delhi, Bangalore, and Ahmedabad. Other centers are either underway or planned in a dozen important locations on the Indian subcontinent.

Śrīla Prabhupāda's most significant contribution, however, is his books. Highly respected by scholars for their authority, depth, and clarity, they are used as textbooks in numerous college courses. His writings have been translated into over fifty languages. The Bhaktivedanta Book Trust, established in 1972 to publish the works of His Divine Grace, has thus become the world's largest publisher of books in the field of Indian religion and philosophy.

In just twelve years, in spite of his advanced age, Śrīla Prabhupāda circled the globe fourteen times on lecture tours that took him to six continents. In spite of such a vigorous schedule, Śrīla Prabhupāda continued to write prolifically. His writings constitute a veritable library of Vedic philosophy, religion, literature, and culture.

An Introduction to ISKCON And Devotee Lifestyle

What Is ISKCON?

The International Society for Krishna Consciousness (ISKCON), popularly known as the Hare Kṛṣṇa movement, is a worldwide association of devotees of Kṛṣṇa, the Supreme Personality of Godhead. God is known by many names, according to His different qualities and activities. In the Bible he is known as Jehovah ("the almighty one"), in the Koran as Allah ("the great one"), and in the *Bhagavad-gītā* as Kṛṣṇa, a Sanskrit name meaning "the all-attractive one."

The movement's main purpose is to promote the well-being of human society by teaching the science of God consciousness (Kṛṣṇa consciousness) according to the timeless Vedic scriptures of India.

Many leading figures in the international religious and academic community have affirmed the movement's authenticity. Diana L. Eck, professor of comparative religion and Indian studies at Harvard University, describes the movement as "a tradition that commands a respected place in the religious life of humankind."

In 1965, His Divine Grace A. C. Bhaktivedanta Swami, known to his followers as Śrīla Prabhupāda, brought Kṛṣṇa consciousness to America. On the day he landed in Boston, on his way to New York City, he penned these words in his diary: "My dear Lord Kṛṣṇa, I am sure that when this transcendental message penetrates [the hearts of the Westerners], they will certainly feel gladdened and thus become liberated from all unhappy conditions of life." He was sixty-nine years old, alone and with few resources, but the wealth of spiritual knowledge and devotion he possessed was an unwavering source of strength and inspiration.

"At a very advanced age, when most people would be resting

on their laurels," writes Harvey Cox, Harvard University theologian and author, "Śrīla Prabhupāda harkened to the mandate of his own spiritual teacher and set out on the difficult and demanding voyage to America. Śrīla Prabhupāda is, of course, only one of thousands of teachers. But in another sense, he is one in a thousand, maybe one in a million."

In 1966, Śrīla Prabhupāda founded the International Society for Krishna Consciousness, which became the formal name for the Hare Kṛṣṇa movement.

Astonishing Growth

In the years that followed, Śrīla Prabhupāda gradually attracted tens of thousands of followers, started more than a hundred temples and ashrams, and published scores of books. His achievement is remarkable in that he transplanted India's ancient spiritual culture to the twentieth-century Western world.

New devotees of Kṛṣṇa soon became highly visible in all the major cities around the world by their public chanting and their distribution of Śrīla Prabhupāda's books of Vedic knowledge. They began staging joyous cultural festivals throughout the year and serving millions of plates of delicious vegetarian food offered to Kṛṣṇa (known as *prasādam*). As a result, ISKCON has significantly influenced the lives of millions of people. In the early 1980's the late A. L. Basham, one of the world's leading authorities on Indian history and culture, wrote, "The Hare Kṛṣṇa movement arose out of next to nothing in less than twenty years and has become known all over the West. This is an important fact in the history of the Western world."

Five Thousand Years of Spiritual Wisdom

Scholars worldwide have acclaimed Śrīla Prabhupāda's translations of Vedic literature. Garry Gelade, a professor at Oxford University's Department of Philosophy, wrote of them: "These texts are to be treasured. No one of whatever faith or philosophical persuasion who reads these books with an open mind can fail to be moved and impressed." And Dr. Larry Shinn,

Dean of the College of Arts and Sciences at Bucknell University, wrote, "Prabhupāda's personal piety gave him real authority. He exhibited complete command of the scriptures, an unusual depth of realization, and an outstanding personal example, because he actually lived what he taught."

The best known of the Vedic texts, the *Bhagavad-gītā* ("Song of God"), is the philosophical basis for the Hare Kṛṣṇa movement. Dating back 5,000 years, it is sacred to nearly a billion people today. This exalted work has been praised by scholars and leaders the world over. Mahatma Gandhi said, "When doubts haunt me, when disappointments stare me in the face and I see not one ray of hope, I turn to the *Bhagavad-gītā* and find a verse to comfort me." Ralph Waldo Emerson wrote, "It was the first of books; it was as if an empire spoke to us, nothing small or unworthy, but large, serene, consistent, the voice of an old intelligence which in another age and climate had pondered and thus disposed of the same questions which exercise us." It is not surprising to anyone familiar with the *Gītā* that Henry David Thoreau said, "In the morning I bathe my intellect in the stupendous and cosmogonal philosophy of the *Bhagavad-gītā*."

As Dr. Shinn pointed out, Śrīla Prabhupāda's *Bhagavad-gītā* (titled *Bhagavad-gītā As It Is*) possesses unique authority not only because of his erudition but because he lived what he taught. Thus unlike the many other English translations of the *Gītā* that preceded his, which is replete with extensive commentary, Śrīla Prabhupāda's has sparked a spiritual revolution throughout the world.

Lord Kṛṣṇa teaches in the *Bhagavad-gītā* that we are not these temporary material bodies but spirit souls, or conscious entities, and that we can find genuine peace and happiness only in spiritual devotion to Him, the Supreme Personality of Godhead.

A Sixteenth-Century Incarnation of Kṛṣṇa

Lord Śrī Caitanya Mahāprabhu, a sixteenth-century full incarnation of Kṛṣṇa, popularized the chanting of God's names all over India. He constantly sang these names of God, as prescribed in the Vedic literatures: Hare Kṛṣṇa, Hare Kṛṣṇa, Kṛṣṇa Kṛṣṇa, Hare Hare/ Hare Rāma, Hare Rāma, Rāma Rāma, Hare Hare. This Hare Kṛṣṇa chant, or *mantra,* is a transcendental sound vibration. It purifies the mind and awakens the dormant love of God that resides in the hearts of all living beings. Lord Caitanya requested His followers to spread the chanting to every town and village of the world.

Anyone can take part in the chanting of the Hare Kṛṣṇa *mantra* and learn the science of spiritual devotion by studying the *Bhagavad-gītā As It Is.* This easy and practical process of self-realization will awaken our natural state of peace and happiness.

Kṛṣṇa Consciousness at Home

by Mahātmā dāsa

In *Dharma: The Way of Transcendence* Śrīla Prabhupāda makes it clear how important it is for everyone to practice Kṛṣṇa consciousness, devotional service to Lord Kṛṣṇa. Of course, living in the association of Kṛṣṇa's devotees in a temple or *āśrama* makes it easier to practice devotional service. But if you're determined, you can follow at home the teachings of Kṛṣṇa consciousness and thus convert your home into a temple.

Spiritual life, like material life, means practical activity. The difference is that whereas we perform material activities for the benefit of ourselves or those we consider ours, we perform spiritual activities for the benefit of Lord Kṛṣṇa, under the guidance of the scriptures and the spiritual master. The key is to accept the guidance of the scripture and the guru. Kṛṣṇa declares in the *Bhagavad-gītā* that a person can achieve neither happiness nor the supreme destination of life—going back to Godhead, back to Lord Kṛṣṇa—if he or she does not follow the injunctions of the scriptures. And *how* to follow the scriptural rules by engaging in practical service to the Lord—that is explained by a bona fide spiritual master. Without following the instructions of a spiritual master who is in an authorized chain of disciplic succession coming from Kṛṣṇa Himself, we cannot make spiritual progress. The practices outlined here are the timeless practices of *bhakti-yoga* as given by the foremost spiritual master and exponent of Kṛṣṇa consciousness in our time, His Divine Grace A. C. Bhaktivedanta Swami Prabhupāda, founder-*ācārya* of the International Society for Krishna Consciousness (ISKCON).

The purpose of spiritual knowledge is to bring us closer to God, or Kṛṣṇa. Kṛṣṇa says in the *Bhagavad-gītā* (18.55), *bhaktyā māṁ abhijānāti:* "I can be known only by devotional service." Knowledge guides us in proper action. Spiritual knowledge directs us to satisfy the desires of Kṛṣṇa through practical engagements in His loving service. Without practical application, theoretical knowledge is of little value.

Spiritual knowledge is meant to direct us in all aspects of life. We should endeavor, therefore, to organize our lives in such a way as to follow Kṛṣṇa's teachings as far as possible. We should try to do our best, to do more than is simply convenient. Then it will be possible for us to rise to the transcendental plane of Kṛṣṇa consciousness, even while living far from a temple.

Chanting the Hare Kṛṣṇa Mantra

The first principle in devotional service is to chant the Hare Kṛṣṇa *mahā-mantra* (*mahā* means "great"; *mantra* means "sound that liberates the mind from ignorance"):

Hare Kṛṣṇa, Hare Kṛṣṇa, Kṛṣṇa Kṛṣṇa, Hare Hare
Hare Rāma, Hare Rāma, Rāma Rāma, Hare Hare

You can chant these holy names of the Lord anywhere and at any time, but it is best to set a specific time of the day to regularly chant. Early morning hours are ideal.

The chanting can be done in two ways: singing the *mantra,* called *kīrtana* (usually done in a group), and saying the *mantra* to oneself, called *japa* (which literally means "to speak softly"). Concentrate on hearing the sound of the holy names. As you chant, pronounce the names clearly and distinctly, addressing Kṛṣṇa in a prayerful mood. When your mind wanders, bring it back to the sound of the Lord's names. Chanting is a prayer to Kṛṣṇa that means "O energy of the Lord [Hare], O all-attractive Lord [Kṛṣṇa], O Supreme Enjoyer [Rāma], please engage me in Your service." The more attentively and sincerely you chant these names of God, the more spiritual progress you will make.

Since God is all-powerful and all-merciful, He has kindly made it very easy for us to chant His names, and He has also invested all His powers in them. Therefore the names of God and God Himself are identical. This means that when we chant the holy names of Kṛṣṇa and Rāma we are directly associating with God and being purified. Therefore we should always try to chant with devotion and reverence. The Vedic literature states that Lord Kṛṣṇa is personally dancing on your tongue when you chant His holy name.

When you chant alone, it is best to chant on *japa* beads (provided in the Mantra Meditation Kit, which is available in the advertisement section at the end of this book). This not only helps you fix your attention on the holy name, but it also helps you count the number of times you chant the *mantra* daily. Each strand of *japa* beads contains 108 small beads and one large bead, the head bead. Begin on a bead next to the head bead and gently roll it between the thumb and middle finger of your right hand as you chant the full Hare Kṛṣṇa *mantra.* Then move to the next bead and repeat the process. In this way, chant on each of the 108 beads until you reach the head bead again. This is one round of *japa*. Then, without chanting on the head bead, reverse the beads and start your second round on the last bead you chanted on.

Initiated devotees vow before the spiritual master to chant at least sixteen rounds of the Hare Kṛṣṇa *mantra* daily. But even if you can chant only one round a day, the principle is that once you commit yourself to chanting that round, you should try complete it every day without fail. When you feel you can chant more, then increase the minimum number of rounds you chant each day—but don't fall below that number. You can chant more than your fixed number, but you should maintain a set minimum each day. (Please note that the beads are sacred and therefore should never touch the ground or be put in an unclean place. To keep your beads clean, it's best to carry them in a special bead bag, such as the one that comes as part of the Mantra Meditation Kit.)

Aside from chanting *japa,* you can also sing the Lord's holy names in *kīrtana*. While you can perform *kīrtana* individually, it is generally performed with others. A melodious *kīrtana* with family or friends is sure to enliven everyone. ISKCON devotees use traditional melodies and instruments, especially in the temple, but you can chant to any melody and use any musical instruments to accompany your chanting. As Lord Caitanya said, "There are no hard and fast rules for chanting Hare Kṛṣṇa." One thing you might want to do, however, is order some *kīrtana* and *japa* audiotapes (see ads).

Setting Up Your Altar

You will likely find that your *japa* and *kīrtana* are especially effective when done before an altar. Lord Kṛṣṇa and His pure devotees are so kind that they allow us to worship them even through their pictures. It is something like mailing a letter: You cannot mail a letter by placing it in just any box; you must use the mailbox authorized by the government. Similarly, we cannot imagine a picture of God and worship that, but we can worship the authorized picture of God, and Kṛṣṇa accepts our worship through that picture.

Setting up an altar at home means receiving the Lord and His pure devotees as your most honored guests. Where should you set up the altar? Well, how would you seat a guest? An ideal place would be clean, well lit, and free from drafts and household disturbances. Your guest, of course, would need a comfortable chair, but for the picture of Kṛṣṇa's form a wall shelf, a mantelpiece, a corner table, or the top shelf of a bookcase will do. You wouldn't seat a guest in your home and then ignore him; you'd provide a place for yourself to sit, too, where you could comfortably face him and enjoy his company. So don't make your altar inaccessible.

What do you need for an altar? Here are the essentials:

1. A picture of Śrīla Prabhupāda.
2. A picture of Lord Caitanya and His associates.
3. A picture of Śrī Śrī Rādhā-Kṛṣṇa.

In addition, you may want an altar cloth, water cups (one for each picture), candles with holders, a special plate for offering food, a small bell, incense, an incense holder, and fresh flowers, which you may offer in vases or simply place before each picture. If you're interested in more elaborate Deity worship, ask any of the ISKCON devotees or write to the BBT (see order form in the back of this book).

The first person we worship on the altar is the spiritual master. The spiritual master is not God. Only God is God. But because the spiritual master is His dearmost servant, God has empowered him, and therefore he deserves the same respect as that given to God. He links the disciple with God and teaches him the process of *bhakti-yoga.* He is God's ambassador to the material world. When a president sends an ambassador to a foreign country, the ambassador receives the same respect as that accorded the president, and the ambassador's words are as authoritative as the president's. Similarly, we should respect the spiritual master as we would God, and revere his words as we would His.

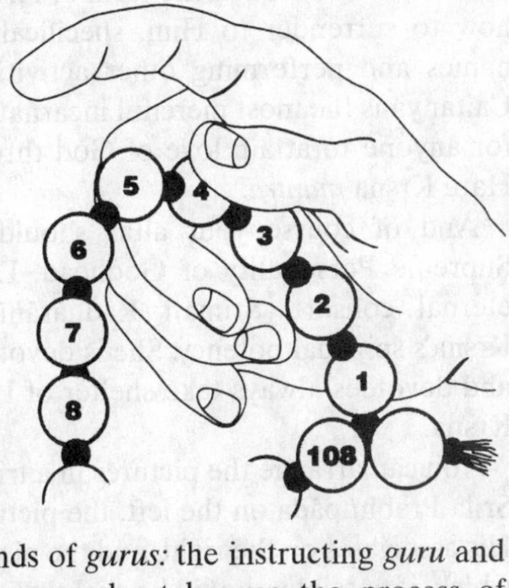

There are two main kinds of *gurus:* the instructing *guru* and the initiating *guru.* Everyone who takes up the process of *bhakti-yoga* as a result of coming in contact with ISKCON owes an immense debt of gratitude to Śrīla Prabhupāda. Before Śrīla

Prabhupāda left India in 1965 to spread Kṛṣṇa consciousness abroad, almost no one outside India knew anything about the practice of pure devotional service to Lord Kṛṣṇa. Therefore, everyone who has learned of the process through his books, his *Back to Godhead* magazine, his tapes, or contact with his followers should offer respect to Śrīla Prabhupāda. As the founder and spiritual guide of the International Society for Krishna Consciousness, he is the instructing *guru* of us all.

As you progress in *bhakti-yoga,* you may eventually want to accept initiation. Before he left this world in 1977, Śrīla Prabhupāda encouraged his qualified disciples to carry on his work by initiating disciples of their own in accordance with his instructions. At present there are many spiritual masters in ISKCON. To learn how you can get in touch with them for spiritual guidance, ask a devotee at your nearby temple, or write to one of the ISKCON centers listed at the end of this book.

The second picture on your altar should be one of the *pañca-tattva,* Lord Caitanya and His four leading associates. Lord Caitanya is the incarnation of God for this age. He is Kṛṣṇa Himself, descended in the form of His own devotee to teach us how to surrender to Him, specifically by chanting His holy names and performing other activities of *bhakti-yoga.* Lord Caitanya is the most merciful incarnation, for He makes it easy for anyone to attain love of God through the chanting of the Hare Kṛṣṇa *mantra.*

And of course your altar should have a picture of the Supreme Personality of Godhead, Lord Śrī Kṛṣṇa, with His eternal consort, Śrīmatī Rādhārāṇī. Śrīmatī Rādhārāṇī is Kṛṣṇa's spiritual potency. She is devotional service personified, and devotees always take shelter of Her to learn how to serve Kṛṣṇa.

You can arrange the pictures in a triangle, with the picture of Śrīla Prabhupāda on the left, the picture of Lord Caitanya and His associates on the right, and the picture of Rādhā and Kṛṣṇa, which, if possible, should be slightly larger than the others, on a small raised platform behind and in the center. Or you can hang the picture of Rādhā and Kṛṣṇa on the wall above.

Carefully clean the altar each morning. Cleanliness is essential in Deity worship. Remember, you wouldn't neglect to clean the room of an important guest, and when you establish an altar you invite Kṛṣṇa and His pure devotees to reside as the most exalted guests in your home. If you have water cups, rinse them out and fill them with fresh water daily. Then place them conveniently close to the pictures. You should remove flowers in vases as soon as they're slightly wilted, or daily if you've offered them at the base of the pictures. You should offer fresh incense at least once a day, and, if possible, light candles and place them near the pictures when you're chanting before the altar.

Please try the things we've suggested so far. It's very simple, really: If you try to love God, you'll gradually realize how much He loves you. That's the essence of *bhakti-yoga.*

Prasādam: How to Eat Spiritually

By His immense transcendental energies, Kṛṣṇa can actually convert matter into spirit. If we place an iron rod in a fire, before long the rod becomes red hot and acts just like fire. In the same way, food prepared for and offered to Kṛṣṇa with love and devotion becomes completely spiritualized. Such food is called Kṛṣṇa *prasādam,* which means "the mercy of Lord Kṛṣṇa."

Eating *prasādam* is a fundamental practice of *bhakti-yoga.* In other forms of yoga one must artificially repress the senses, but the *bhakti-yogī* can engage his or her senses in a variety of pleasing spiritual activities, such as tasting delicious food offered to Lord Kṛṣṇa. In this way the senses gradually become spiritualized and bring the devotee more and more transcendental pleasure by being engaged in devotional service. Such spiritual pleasure far surpasses any material experience.

Lord Caitanya said of *prasādam,* "Everyone has tasted these foods before. However, now that they have been prepared for Kṛṣṇa and offered to Him with devotion, these foods have acquired extraordinary tastes and uncommon fragrances. Just taste them and see the difference in the experience! Apart from the taste, even the fragrance pleases the mind and makes one forget any other fragrance. Therefore, it should be understood that the spiritual nectar of Kṛṣṇa's lips must have touched these ordinary foods and imparted to them all their transcendental qualities."

Eating only food offered to Kṛṣṇa is the perfection of vegetarianism. In itself, being a vegetarian is not enough; after all, even pigeons and monkeys are vegetarians. But when we go beyond vegetarianism to a diet of *prasādam,* our eating becomes helpful in achieving the goal of human life—reawakening the soul's original relationship with God. In the *Bhagavad-gītā* Lord Kṛṣṇa says that unless one eats only food that has been offered to Him in sacrifice, one will suffer the reactions of *karma.*

How to Prepare and Offer Prasādam

As you walk down the supermarket aisles selecting the foods you will offer to Kṛṣṇa, you need to know what is offerable and what is not. In the *Bhagavad-gītā,* Lord Kṛṣṇa states, "If one offers Me with love and devotion a leaf, a flower, a fruit, or water, I will accept it." From this verse it is understood that we can offer Kṛṣṇa foods prepared from milk products, vegetables, fruits, nuts, and grains. (See the ads for some of the many Hare

Kṛṣṇa cookbooks.) Meat, fish, and eggs are not offerable. And a few vegetarian items are also forbidden—garlic and onions, for example, which are in the mode of darkness. (*Hing,* or asafetida, is a tasty substitute for them in cooking and is available at most Indian groceries and ISKCON temple stores.) Nor can you offer to Kṛṣṇa coffee or tea that contain caffeine. If you like these beverages, purchase caffeine-free coffee and herbal teas.

While shopping, be aware that you may find meat, fish, and egg products mixed with other foods; so be sure to read labels carefully. For instance, some brands of yogurt and sour cream contain gelatin, a substance made from the horns, hooves, and bones of slaughtered animals. Also, make sure the cheese you buy contains no animal rennet, an enzyme extracted from the stomach tissues of slaughtered calves. Most hard cheese sold in America contains this rennet, so be careful about any cheese you can't verify as being free from animal rennet.

Also avoid foods cooked by nondevotees. According to the subtle laws of nature, the cook acts upon the food not only physically but mentally as well. Food thus becomes an agent for subtle influences on your consciousness. The principle is the same as that at work with a painting: a painting is not simply a collection of strokes on a canvas but an expression of the artist's state of mind, which affects the viewer. So if you eat food cooked by nondevotees—employees working in a factory, for example—then you're sure to absorb a dose of materialism and *karma.* So as far as possible use only fresh, natural ingredients.

In preparing food, cleanliness is the most important principle. Nothing impure should be offered to God; so keep your kitchen very clean. Always wash your hands thoroughly before entering the kitchen. While preparing food, do not taste it, for you are cooking the meal not for yourself but for the pleasure of Kṛṣṇa. Arrange portions of the food on dinnerware kept especially for this purpose; no one but the Lord should eat from these dishes. The easiest way to offer food is simply to pray, "My dear Lord Kṛṣṇa, please accept this food," and to chant each of the following prayers three times while ringing a bell (see the Sanskrit Pronunciation Guide on page 133):

1. Prayer to Śrīla Prabhupāda:

nama oṁ viṣṇu-pādāya kṛṣṇa-preṣṭhāya bhū-tale
śrīmate bhaktivedānta-svāminn iti nāmine

namas te sārasvate deve gaura-vāṇī-pracāriṇe
nirviśeṣa-śūnyavādi-pāścātya-deśa-tāriṇe

"I offer my respectful obeisances unto His Divine Grace A. C. Bhaktivedanta Swami Prabhupāda, who is very dear to Lord Kṛṣṇa, having taken shelter at His lotus feet. Our respectful obeisances are unto you, O spiritual master, servant of Bhaktisiddhānta Sarasvatī Gosvāmī. You are kindly preaching the message of Lord Caitanyadeva and delivering the Western countries, which are filled with impersonalism and voidism."

2. Prayer to Lord Caitanya:

namo mahā-vadānyāya kṛṣṇa-prema-pradāya te
kṛṣṇāya kṛṣṇa-caitanya-nāmne gaura-tviṣe namaḥ

"O most munificent incarnation! You are Kṛṣṇa Himself appearing as Śrī Kṛṣṇa Caitanya Mahāprabhu. You have assumed the golden color of Śrīmatī Rādhārāṇī, and You are widely distributing pure love of Kṛṣṇa. We offer our respectful obeisances unto You."

3. Prayer to Lord Kṛṣṇa:

namo brahmaṇya-devāya go-brāhmaṇa-hitāya ca
jagad-dhitāya kṛṣṇāya govindāya namo namaḥ

"I offer my respectful obeisances unto Lord Kṛṣṇa, who is the worshipable Deity for all *brāhmaṇas*, the well-wisher of the cows and the *brāhmaṇas,* and the benefactor of the whole world. I offer my repeated obeisances to the Personality of Godhead, known as Kṛṣṇa and Govinda."

Remember that the real purpose of preparing and offering food to the Lord is to show your devotion and gratitude to Him.

Kṛṣṇa accepts your devotion, not the physical offering itself. God is complete in Himself—He doesn't need anything—but out of His immense kindness He allows us to offer food to Him so that we can develop our love for Him.

After offering the food to the Lord, wait at least five minutes for Him to partake of the preparations. Then you should transfer the food from the special dinnerware and wash the dishes and utensils you used for the offering. Now you and any guests may eat the *prasādam.* While you eat, try to appreciate the spiritual value of the food. Remember that because Kṛṣṇa has accepted it, it is nondifferent from Him, and therefore by eating it you will become purified.

Everything you offer on your altar becomes *prasādam,* the mercy of the Lord. Flowers, incense, the water, the food—everything you offer for the Lord's pleasure becomes spiritualized. The Lord enters into the offerings, and thus the remnants are nondifferent from Him. So you should not only deeply respect the things you've offered, but you should distribute them to others as well. Distribution of *prasādam* is an essential part of Deity worship.

Everyday Life: The Four Regulative Principles

Anyone serious about progressing in Kṛṣṇa consciousness must try to avoid the following four sinful activities:

1. **Eating meat, fish, or eggs.** These foods are saturated with the modes of passion and ignorance and therefore cannot be offered to the Lord. A person who eats these foods participates in a conspiracy of violence against helpless animals and thus stops his spiritual progress dead in its tracks.

2. **Gambling.** Gambling invariably puts one into anxiety and fuels greed, envy, and anger.

3. **The use of intoxicants.** Drugs, alcohol, and tobacco, as well as any drinks or foods containing caffeine, cloud the mind, over-

stimulate the senses, and make it impossible to understand or follow the principles of *bhakti-yoga*.

4. **Illicit sex.** This is sex outside of marriage or sex in marriage for any purpose other than procreation. Sex for pleasure compels one to identify with the body and takes one far from Kṛṣṇa consciousness. The scriptures teach that sex is the most powerful force binding us to the material world. Anyone serious about advancing in Kṛṣṇa consciousness should minimize sex or eliminate it entirely.

Engagement in Practical Devotional Service

Everyone must do some kind of work, but if you work only for yourself you must accept the karmic reactions of that work. As Lord Kṛṣṇa says in the *Bhagavad-gītā* (3.9), "Work done as a sacrifice for Viṣṇu [Kṛṣṇa] has to be performed. Otherwise work binds one to the material world."

You needn't change your occupation, except if you're now engaged in a sinful job such as working as a butcher or bartender. If you're a writer, write for Kṛṣṇa; if you're an artist, create for Kṛṣṇa; if you're a secretary, type for Kṛṣṇa. You may also directly help the temple in your spare time, and you should sacrifice some of the fruits of your work by contributing a portion of your earnings to help maintain the temple and propagate Kṛṣṇa consciousness. Some devotees living outside the temple buy Hare Kṛṣṇa literature and distribute it to their friends and associates, or they engage in a variety of services at the temple. There is also a wide network of devotees who gather in each other's homes for chanting, worship, and study. Write to your local temple or the Society's secretary to learn of any such programs near you.

Additional Devotional Principles

There are many more devotional practices that can help you become Kṛṣṇa conscious. Here are two vital ones:

Studying Hare Kṛṣṇa literature. Śrīla Prabhupāda, the founder-*ācārya* of ISKCON, dedicated much of his time to writing books such as the *Bhagavad-gītā* and *Śrīmad-Bhāgavatam,* both of which are quoted extensively in *Dharma: The Way of Transcendence*. Hearing the words—or reading the writings—of a realized spiritual master is an essential spiritual practice. So try to set aside some time every day to read Śrīla Prabhupāda's books. You can get a free catalog of available books and tapes from the BBT.

Associating with devotees. Śrīla Prabhupāda established the Hare Kṛṣṇa movement to give people in general the chance to associate with devotees of the Lord. This is the best way to gain faith in the process of Kṛṣṇa consciousness and become enthusiastic in devotional service. Conversely, maintaining intimate connections with nondevotees slows one's spiritual progress. So try to visit the Hare Kṛṣṇa center nearest you as often as possible.

In Closing

The beauty of Kṛṣṇa consciousness is that you can take as much as you're ready for. Kṛṣṇa Himself promises in the *Bhagavad-gītā* (2.40), "There is no loss or diminution in this endeavor, and even a little advancement on this path protects one from the most fearful type of danger." So bring Kṛṣṇa into your daily life, and we guarantee you'll feel the benefit.

Hare Kṛṣṇa!

Sanskrit Pronunciation Guide

The system of transliteration used in this book conforms to a system that scholars have accepted to indicate the pronunciation of each sound in the Sanskrit language.

The short vowel **a** is pronounced like the **u** in b**u**t, long **ā** like the **a** in f**a**r. Short **i** is pronounced as in p**i**n, long **ī** as in p**i**que, short **u** as in p**u**ll, and long **ū** as in r**u**le. The vowel **ṛ** is pronounced like the **ri** in **ri**m, **e** like the **ey** in th**ey**, **o** like the **o** in g**o**, **ai** like the **ai** in **ai**sle, and **au** like the **ow** in h**ow**. The *anusvāra* (**ṁ**) is pronounced like the **n** in the French word *bo***n**, and *visarga* (**ḥ**) is pronounced as a final **h** sound. At the end of a couplet, **aḥ** is pronounced **aha**, and **iḥ** is pronounced **ihi**.

The guttural consonants—**k, kh, g, gh,** and **ṅ**—are pronounced from the throat in much the same manner as in English. **K** is pronounced as in **k**ite, **kh** as in Ec**kh**art, **g** as in **g**ive, **gh** as in di**g h**ard, and **ṅ** as in si**ng.**

The palatal consonants—**c, ch, j, jh,** and **ñ**—are pronounced with the tongue touching the firm ridge behind the teeth. **C** is pronounced as in **ch**air, **ch** as in staun**ch-h**eart, **j** as in **j**oy, **jh** as in he**dgeh**og, and **ñ** as in ca**ny**on.

The cerebral consonants—**ṭ, ṭh, ḍ, ḍh,** and **ṇ**—are pronounced with the tip of the tongue turned up and drawn back against the dome of the palate. **Ṭ** is pronounced as in **t**ub, **ṭh** as in ligh**t-h**eart, **ḍ** as in **d**ove, **ḍh** as in re**d-h**ot, and **ṇ** as in **n**ut. The dental consonants—**t, th, d, dh,** and **n**—are pronounced in the same manner as the cerebrals, but with the forepart of the tongue against the teeth.

The labial consonants—**p, ph, b, bh,** and **m**—are pronounced with the lips. **P** is pronounced as in **p**ine, **ph** as in u**ph**ill, **b** as in **b**ird, **bh** as in ru**b-h**ard, and **m** as in **m**other.

The semivowels—**y, r, l,** and **v**—are pronounced as in **y**es, **r**un, **l**ight, and **v**ine respectively. The sibilants—**ś, ṣ,** and **s**—are pronounced, respectively, as in the German word **s***prechen* and the English words **sh**ine and **s**un. The letter **h** is pronounced as in **h**ome.

Glossary

A

Absolute—*See:* Absolute Truth.

Absolute Truth—the ultimate source of all energies.

Ācārya—an ideal teacher, who teaches by his personal eample; a spiritual master.

Ahaṅkāra—false ego, by which the soul misidentifies with the material body.

Artha—economic development.

Arjuna—one of the five Pāṇḍava brothers. Kṛṣṇa became his chariot driver and spoke the *Bhagavad-gītā* to him.

Āśrama—one of four spiritual orders of life. *See also: Brahmacarya; Gṛhastha; Vānaprastha; Sannyāsa.*

Asura—a person opposed to the service of the Lord.

B

Battle of Kurukṣetra—a battle between the Kurus and the Pāṇḍavas, which took place five thousand years ago and before which Lord Kṛṣṇa spoke *Bhagavad-gītā* to Arjuna.

Bhagavad-gītā—the discourse between the Supreme Lord, Kṛṣṇa, and His devotee Arjuna epounding devotional service as both the principal means and the ultimate end of spiritual perfection.

Bhagavān—the Supreme Lord, who possesses in full the six opulences of wealth, strength, fame, beauty, knowledge, and renunciation.

Bhāgavata—(1) the *Śrīmad-Bhāgavatam* (*Bhāgavata Purāṇa*); (2) a devotee of the Lord.

Bhakti—devotional service to the Supreme Lord.

Bhakti-yoga—linking with the Supreme Lord through devotional service.

Brahmā—the first created living being and secondary creator of the material universe.

Brahma-bhūta—the joyful state free of material contamination; liberation.

Brahmacārī—one in the first order of spiritual life; a celibate student of a spiritual master.

Brahmacarya—celibate student life; the first order of Vedic spiritual life.

Brahma-jijñāsā—inquiry into the Absolute Truth.

Brahman—(1) the soul; (2) the impersonal, all-pervasive aspect of the Supreme; (3) the Supreme Personality of Godhead; (4) the *mahat-tattva,* or total material substance.

Brāhmaṇa—a person wise in Vedic knowledge, fixed in goodness, and knowledgeable of Brahman, the Absolute Truth; a member of the first Vedic social order.

Brahma-saṁhitā—a very ancient Sanskrit scripture recording the prayers of Brahmā to the Supreme Lord, Govinda.

C

Caitanya-caritāmṛta—a biography of Śrī Caitanya Mahāprabhu composed in Bengali in the late siteenth century by Śrīla Kṛṣṇadāsa Kavirāja.

Caitanya Mahāprabhu (1486–1534)—the Supreme Lord appearing as His own greatest devotee to teach love of God, especially through the process of congregational chanting of His holy names.

Cāṇakya Paṇḍita—the prime minister of King Candragupta. His aphorisms are still famous throughout India.

Candra—the demigod of the moon.

D

Deity of the Lord—the authorized form of Kṛṣṇa worshiped in temples.

Deva—a demigod or godly person.

Dharma—religion; essential characterstic; duty, especially everyone's eternal service nature.

G

Gopīs—Kṛṣṇa's cowherd girlfriends, who are His most surrendered and confidential devotees.

Gosvāmī—a controller of the mind and senses; the title of one in the renounced, or *sannyāsa,* order.

Govinda—the Supreme Lord, Kṛṣṇa, who gives pleasure to the land, the senses, and the cows.

Gṛhastha—regulated householder life; the second order of Vedic spiritual life; one in that order.

Guru—a spiritual master.

H

Haṭha-yoga—the practice of postures and breathing exercises for achieving purification and sense control.

Hindu—a newly-concocted name for members of various social and religious groups of India. The term has no spiritual significance.

Hiraṇyakaśipu—a powerful demon who tormented his son Prahlāda, a great devotee, and was slain by Lord Nṛsiṁhadeva.

I

Indra—the chief of the administrative demigods, king of the heavenly planets, and presiding deity of rain.

Īśopaniṣad—one of the principal *Upaniṣads.*

J

Jagannātha—the Supreme Lord, who is Lord of the universe; the particular Deity form of that Lord at Purī, Orissa.

Jagannātha Purī—a city in Orissa, India, that is home to an ancient temple of the Supreme Lord in a Deity form known as Jagannātha, "Lord of the universe"; each year a massive car festival is held in His honor.

Jñāna-yoga—the path of spiritual realization through a speculative philosophical search for truth.

Jñānī—one who cultivates knowledge by empirical speculation.

K

Kālī—the personified material energy and the wife of Lord Śiva.

Kali-yuga (Age of Kali)—the present age, characterized by quarrel. The last in the cycle of four ages, it began five thousand years ago.

Kāma—lust; material desire in general.

Karma—(1) material action performed according to scriptural regulations; (2) action pertaining to the development of the material body; (3) any material action that will incur a subsequent reaction; (4) the material reaction one incurs due to fruitive activities.

Karma-yoga—the path of God realization through dedicating the fruits of one's work to God.

Karmī—one engaged in karma, fruitive activity; a materialist.

Kṛṣṇa-kathā—discussions by or about the Supreme Lord, Kṛṣṇa.

Kṛṣṇa-prasādam—*See: Prasādam.*

Kṣatriya—a warrior or administrator; the second Vedic social order.

M

Mahābhārata—Vyāsadeva's epic history of greater India, which includes the events of the Kurukṣetra war and the narration of the *Bhagavad-gītā*.

Mahā-mantra—the great chant for deliverance: Hare Kṛṣṇa,

Hare Kṛṣṇa, Kṛṣṇa Kṛṣṇa, Hare Hare/ Hare Rāma, Hare Rāma, Rāma Rāma, Hare Hare.

Mahātmā—a "great soul," an exalted devotee of Lord Kṛṣṇa.

Maṅgala-ārati—the daily predawn worship ceremony honoring the Deity of the Supreme Lord.

Māyā—the inferior, illusory energy of the Supreme Lord, which rules over this material creation; also, forgetfulness of one's relationship with Kṛṣṇa.

Māyāvāda—the impersonal philosophy propounding the unqualified oneness of God and the living entities and the nonreality of manifest nature.

Māyāvādī—an impersonalist philosopher who conceives of the Absolute as ultimately formless and the living entity as equal to God .

Mokṣa—liberation from material bondage.

Mūḍha—a foolish, asslike person.

Mukti—liberation from material bondage.

N

Naimiṣāraṇya—the sacred forest where *Śrīmad-Bhāgavatam* was spoken by Sūta Gosvāmī to a great assembly of sages.

Nārada—*See:* Nārada Muni.

Nārada Muni—a pure devotee of the Lord who travels throughout the universes in his eternal body, glorifying devotional service. He is the spiritual master of Vyāsadeva and of many other great devotees.

Nārada-pañcarātra—Nārada Muni's book on the processes of Deity worship and mantra meditation.

Narottama Dāsa Ṭhākura—an exalted devotee of Lord Caitanya who lived in the sixteenth century and is known especially for his devotional songs written in simple Bengali but containing the highest spiritual truths.

Nivṛtti-mārga—the path of renunciation, which leads to liberation.

P

Pañcarātra—Vedic literatures describing the process of Deity worship. *See also: Nārada-pañcarātra*

Paṇḍita—a scholar.

Paramātmā—the Supersoul, a Viṣṇu expansion of the Supreme Lord residing in the heart of each embodied living entity and pervading all of material nature.

Paramparā—a disciplic succession.

Parīkṣit Mahārāja—the emperor of the world who heard *Śrīmad-Bhāgavatam* from Śukadeva Gosvāmī and thus attained perfection.

Prakṛti—the energy of the Supreme; the female principle enjoyed by the male *puruṣa*.

Prasādam—the Lord's mercy; food or other items spiritualized by being first offered to the Supreme Lord.

Pravṛtti-mārga—the path of sense enjoyment in accordance with Vedic regulations.

Prema—pure love of God, the highest stage in the progressive development of devotional service.

Purāṇas—eighteen literary supplements to the *Vedas,* discussing such topics as the creation of the universe, incarnations of the Supreme Lord and demigods, and the history of dynasties of saintly kings.

Purī—*See:* Jagannātha Purī.

R

Rādhārāṇī—Lord Kṛṣṇa's most intimate consort, who is the personification of His internal, spiritual potency.

Regulative principles (four)—(1) no meat-eating; (2) no illicit sex; (3) no intoxication; (4) no gambling.

Ṛṣabhadeva—an incarnation of the Supreme Lord as a devotee king who, after instructing his sons in spiritual life, renounced His kingdom for a life of austerity.

Rūpa Gosvāmī—the chief of the six Vaiṣṇava spiritual masters who directly followed Lord Caitanya Mahāprabhu and systematically presented His teachings.

S

Samādhi—trance; complete absorption in God consciousness.

Sanātana Gosvāmī—one of the six Vaiṣṇava spiritual masters who directly followed Lord Caitanya Mahāprabhu and systematically presented His teachings.

Sannyāsa—renounced life; the fourth order of Vedic spiritual life.

Sannyāsī—one in the *sannyāsa* (renounced) order.

Śāstra—revealed scripture, such as the Vedic literature.

Śikṣāṣṭaka—eight verses by Lord Caitanya Mahāprabhu glorifying the chanting of the Lord's holy name.

Śiva—the special incarnation of the Lord as the demigod in charge of the mode of ignorance and the destruction of the material manifestation.

Smṛti—revealed scriptures supplementary to the *śruti,* or original Vedic scriptures, which are the *Vedas* and *Upaniṣads.*

Śrīmad-Bhāgavatam—the *Purāṇa,* or history, written by Śrīla Vyāsadeva specifically give a deep understanding of Lord Kṛṣṇa, His devotees, and devotional service.

Śruti—knowledge via hearing; also, the original Vedic scriptures (the *Vedas* and *Ūpaniṣads*), given directly by the Supreme Lord.

Śūdra—a laborer; the fourth of the Vedic social orders.

Śukadeva Gosvāmī—the great devotee sage who spoke *Śrīmad-Bhāgavatam* to King Parīkṣit just prior to the King's death.

Sūta Gosvāmī—the great devotee sage who recounted the discourses between Parīkṣit and Śukadeva to the sages assembled in the forest of Naimiṣāraṇya.

Sūrya—the demigod of the sun.

Svargaloka—the heavenly planets of the material world.

T

Tapasya—austerity; accepting some voluntary inconvenience for a higher purpose.

U

Upadeśāmṛta—a short Sanskrit work by Rūpa Gosvāmī containing important instructions about devotional service to Lord Kṛṣṇa.

Upaniṣads—108 philosophical works that appear within the *Vedas*.

V

Vaiṣṇava—a devotee of Lord Viṣṇu, or Kṛṣṇa.

Vaiśya—a farmer or merchant; the third Vedic social order.

Vānaprastha—one who has retired from family life; the third order of Vedic spiritual life.

Varṇas—the four Vedic social-occupational divisions of society, distinguished by quality of work and situation in the modes of nature (*guṇas*). *See also: Brāhmaṇa; Kṣatriya; Vaiśya;* and *Śūdra.*

Varṇāśrama-dharma—the Vedic social system of four social and four spiritual orders. *See also: Varṇa; Āśrama*

Vedānta-śruti—*See: Vedānta-sūtra.*

Vedānta-sūtra—the philosophical treatise written by Vyāsadeva, consisting of aphorisms that embody the essential meaning of the *Upaniṣads.*

Vedas—the four original revealed scriptures (*Ṛg, Sāma, Atharva,* and *Yajur*).

Vedic—pertaining to a culture in which all aspects of human life are under the guidance of the *Vedas*.

Virāṭ-puruṣa—the "universal form" of the Supreme Lord, conceived of as the totality of all material manifestations.

Viṣṇu(s)—the Supreme Lord; Lord Kṛṣṇa's expansions in Vaikuṇṭha and for the creation and maintenance of the material universes.

Vivasvān—the demigod in charge of the sun.

Vṛndāvana—Kṛṣṇa's eternal abode, where He fully manifests His quality of sweetness; the village on this earth in which He enacted His childhood pastimes five thousand years ago.

Vyāsadeva—the incarnation of Lord Kṛṣṇa who gave the *Vedas, Purāṇas, Vedānta-sūtra,* and *Mahābhārata* to mankind.

Y

Yoga—spiritual discipline undergone to link oneself with the Supreme.

Yogi—a transcendentalist striving for union with the Supreme.

The International Society for Krishna Consciousness
Founder-Ācārya: His Divine Grace A.C. Bhaktivedanta Swami Prabhupāda

CENTERS AROUND THE WORLD

NORTH AMERICA

CANADA

Calgary, Alberta — 313 Fourth Street N.E., T2E 3S3/ Tel. (403) 265-3302

Edmonton, Alberta — 9353 35th Avenue, T6E 5R5/ Tel. (403) 439-9999

Montreal, Quebec — 1626 Pie IX Boulevard, H1V 2C5/ Tel. (514) 521-1301

Ottawa, Ontario — 212 Somerset St. E., K1N 6V4/ Tel. (613) 565-6544

Regina, Saskatchewan — 1279 Retallack St., S4T 2H8/ Tel. (306) 525-1640

Toronto, Ontario — 243 Avenue Rd., M5R 2J6/ Tel. (416) 922-5415

Vancouver, B.C. — 5462 S.E. Marine Dr., Burnaby V5J 3G8/ Tel. (604) 433-9728

Victoria, B.C. — 1350 Lang St., V8T 2S5/ Tel. (604) 920-0026

FARM COMMUNITY

Ashcroft, B.C. — Saranagati Dhama, Box 99, V0K 1A0

ADDITIONAL RESTAURANT

Vancouver — Hare Krishna Place, 46 Begbie St., New Westminster

U.S.A.

Atlanta, Georgia — 1287 South Ponce de Leon Ave. N.E., 30306/ Tel. (404) 378-9234

Austin, Texas — 807-A E. 30th St., 78705/ Tel. (512) 320-0477/ E-mail: sankarsana@aol.com

Baltimore, Maryland — 200 Bloomsbury Ave., Catonsville, 21228/ Tel. (410) 744-1624 or 4069

Boise, Idaho — 1615 Martha St., 83706/ Tel. (208) 344-4274

Boston, Massachusetts — 72 Commonwealth Ave., 02116/ Tel. (617) 247-8611

Chicago, Illinois — 1716 W. Lunt Ave., 60626/ Tel. (312) 973-0900

Columbus, Ohio — 379 W. Eighth Ave., 43201/ Tel. (614) 421-1661

Dallas, Texas — 5430 Gurley Ave., 75223/ Tel. (214) 827-6330

Denver, Colorado — 1400 Cherry St., 80220/ Tel. (303) 333-5461

Detroit, Michigan — 383 Lenox Ave., 48215/ Tel. (313) 824-6000

Gainesville, Florida — 214 N.W. 14th St., 32603/ Tel. (904) 336-4183

Gurabo, Puerto Rico — HC01-Box 8440, 00778-9763/ Tel. (809) 737-1658

Hartford, Connecticut — 1683 Main St., E. Hartford, 06108/ Tel. (860) 289-7252

Honolulu, Hawaii — 51 Coelho Way, 96817/ Tel. (808) 595-3947

Houston, Texas — 1320 W. 34th St., 77018/ Tel. (713) 686-4482

Laguna Beach, California — 285 Legion St., 92651/ Tel. (714) 494-7029

Long Island, New York — 197 S. Ocean Avenue, Freeport, 11520/ Tel. (516) 223-4909

Los Angeles, California — 3764 Watseka Ave., 90034/ Tel. (310) 836-2676

Miami, Florida — 3220 Virginia St., 33133 (mail: P.O. Box 337, Coconut Grove, FL 33233)/Tel. (305) 442-7218

New Orleans, Louisiana — 2936 Esplanade Ave., 70119/ Tel. (504) 486-3583

New York, New York — 305 Schermerhorn St., Brooklyn, 11217/ Tel. (718) 855-6714

New York, New York — 26 Second Avenue, 10003/ Tel. (212) 420-1130

Philadelphia, Pennsylvania — 41 West Allens Lane, 19119/ Tel. (215) 247-4600

Phoenix, Arizona — 100 S. Weber Dr., Chandler, 85226/ Tel. (602) 705-4900/ Fax: (602) 705-4901

Portland, Oregon — 5137 N.E. 42 Ave., 97218/ Tel. (503) 287-3252

St. Louis, Missouri — 3926 Lindell Blvd., 63108/ Tel. (314) 535-8085

San Diego, California — 1030 Grand Ave., Pacific Beach, 92109/ Tel. (619) 483-2500

Seattle, Washington — 1420 228th Ave. S.E., Issaquah, 98027/ Tel. (206) 391-3293

Tallahassee, Florida — 1323 Nylic St. (mail: P.O. Box 20224, 32304)/ Tel. (904) 681-9258

Towaco, New Jersey — P.O. Box 109, 07082/ Tel. (201) 299-0970

Tucson, Arizona — 711 E. Blacklidge Dr., 85719/ Tel. (520) 792-0630

Washington, D.C. — 3200 Ivy Way, Harwood, MD 20776/ Tel. (301) 261-4493

Washington, D.C. — 10310 Oaklyn Dr., Potomac, Maryland 20854/ Tel. (301) 299-2100

FARM COMMUNITIES

Alachua, Florida (New Raman Reti) — P.O. Box 819, 32615/ Tel. (904) 462-2017

Carriere, Mississippi (New Talavan) — 31492 Anner Road, 39426/ Tel. (601) 799-1354

Gurabo, Puerto Rico (New Govardhana Hill) — (contact ISKCON Gurabo)

Hillsborough, North Carolina (New Goloka) — 1032 Dimmocks Mill Rd., 27278/ Tel. (919) 732-6492

Moundsville, West Virginia (New Vrindaban) — R.D. No. 1, Box 319, Hare Krishna Ridge, 26042/ Tel. (304) 843-1600/ Fax: (304) 845-9819/ E-mail: story 108@juno.com; (lodging:) kisore@aol.com

Mulberry, Tennessee (Murari-sevaka) — Rt. No. 1, Box 146-A, 37359/ Tel (615) 759-6888

Port Royal, Pennsylvania (Gita Nagari) — R.D. No. 1, Box 839, 17082/ Tel. (717) 527-4101

ADDITIONAL RESTAURANTS AND DINING

Boise, Idaho — Govinda's, 500 W. Main St., 83702/ Tel. (208) 338-9710

Eugene, Oregon — Govinda's Vegetarian Buffet, 270 W. 8th St., 97401/ Tel. (503) 686-3531

Fresno, California — Govinda's, 2373 E. Shaw, 93710/ Tel. (209) 225-1230

Gainesville, Florida — Radha's, 125 NW 23rd Ave., 32609/ Tel. (904) 376-9012

EUROPE

UNITED KINGDOM AND IRELAND

Belfast, Northern Ireland — 140 Upper Dunmurray Lane, BT17 OHE/ Tel. +44 (01232) 620530

Birmingham, England — 84 Stanmore Rd., Edgebaston, B16 9TB/ Tel. +44 (0121) 420-4999
Coventry, England — Sri Sri Radha Krishna Cultural Centre, Kingfield Rd., Radford (mail: 19 Gloucester St., CV1 3BZ)/ Tel. +44 (01203) 555420
Dublin, Ireland — 56 Dame St., Dublin 2/ Tel. +353 (01) 679-1306
Glasgow, Scotland — Karuna Bhavan, Bankhouse Rd., Lesmahagow, Lanarkshire ML11 0ES/Tel. +44 (01555) 894790
Leicester, England — 21 Thoresby St., North Evington, Leicester LE5 4GU/Tel. +44 (0116) 2762587 or 2367723
Liverpool, England — 114A Bold St., Liverpool L1 4HY/ Tel. +44 (0151) 708 9400
London, England (city) — 10 Soho St., London W1V 5DA/ Tel. +44 (0171) 4373662 (business hours), 4393606 (other times); Govinda's Restaurant: 4374928
London, England (country) — Bhaktivedanta Manor, Letchmore Heath, Watford, Hertfordshire WD2 8EP/ Tel. +44 (01923) 857244
London, England (south) — 42 Enmore Road, South Norwood, London SE25/ Tel. +44 (0181) 656-4296
Manchester, England — 20 Mayfield Rd., Whalley Range, Manchester M16 8FT/ Tel. +44 (0161) 2264416
Newcastle upon Tyne, England — 21 Leazes Park Rd., NE1 4PF/ Tel. +44 (0191) 2220150

FARM COMMUNITIES

County Wicklow, Ireland — Rathgorragh, Kiltegan/ Tel. +353 508-73305
Lisnaskea, North Ireland — Hare Krishna Island, BT92 9GN Lisnaskea, Co. Fremanagh/Tel. +44 (03657) 21512
London, England — (contact Bhaktivedanta Manor)

ADDITIONAL RESTAURANT

Manchester, England — Krishna's, 20 Cyril St., Manchester 14/ Tel. +44 (0161) 226 965
(Krishna conscious programs are held regularly in more than twenty other cities in the U.K. For information, contact Bhaktivedanta Books Ltd., Reader Services Dept., P.O. Box 324, Borehamwood, Herts WD6 1NB/ Tel. +44 [0181] 905-1244.)

GERMANY

Abentheuer — Bockingstr 8, 55767 Abentheuer/ Tel. +49 (06782) 6364
Berlin — Johannisthaler Chaussee 78, 12259 Berlin (Britz)/ Tel. +49 (030) 613 2400
Boeblingen — Friedrich-List Strasse 58, 71032 Boeblingen/ Tel. +49 (07031) 22 33 98
Cologne — Taunusstr. 40, 51105 Köln/ Tel. +49 (0221) 830 3778
Flensburg— Hoerup 1, 24980 Neuhoerup/ Tel. +49 (04639) 73 36
Hamburg — Muehlenstr. 93, 25421 Pinneberg/ Tel. +49 (04101) 2 39 31
Hannover — Zeiss Strasse 21, 30519 Hannover/ Tel. +49 (0511) 83 74 31
Heidelberg — Kurfürsten-Anlage 5, D-69115 Heidelberg/ Tel. +49 (06221) 16 51 01
Munich — Tal 38, 80331 Munchen/ Tel +49 (089) 29 23 17
Nuremberg — Kopernikusplatz 12, 90459 Nürnberg/ Tel. +49 (0911) 45 32 86
Wiesbaden — Schiersteiner Strasse 6, 65187 Wiesbaden/ Tel. +49 (0611) 37 33 12

FARM COMMUNITY

Jandelsbrunn — Nava Jiyada Nrsimha Ksetra, Zielberg 20, 94118 Jandelsbrunn/ Tel +49 (08583) 316

ADDITIONAL RESTAURANT

Berlin — Higher Taste, Kurfuerstendamm 157/158, 10709 Berlin/ Tel. +49 (030) 892 99 17

ITALY

Asti — Roatto, Frazione Valle Reale 20/ Tel. +39 (0141) 938406
Bergamo — Villaggio Hare Krishna, Via Galileo Galilei 41, 24040 Chignolo D'isola (BG)/Tel. +39 (035) 4940706
Bologna — Via Ramo Barchetta 2, 40010 Bentivoglio (BO)/ Tel. +39 (051) 863924
Catania — Via San Nicolo al Borgo 28, 95128 Catania, Sicily/ Tel. +39 (095) 522-252
Naples — Via Vesuvio, N33, Ercolano LNA7/ Tel. +39 (081) 739-0398
Rome — Nepi, Sri Gaura Mandala, Via Mazzanese Km. 0,700 (dalla Cassia uscita Calcata), Pian del Pavone (Viterbo)/ Tel. +39 (0761) 527038
Vicenza — Via Roma 9, 36020 Albettone (Vicenza)/ Tel. +39 (0444) 790573 or 790566

FARM COMMUNITY

Florence (Villa Vrindavan) — Via Communale degli Scopeti 108, S. Andrea in Percussina, San Casciano, Val di Pesa (FI) 5002/ Tel. +39 (055) 820-054

ADDITIONAL RESTAURANT

Milan — Govinda's, Via Valpetrosa 3/5, 20123 Milano/ Tel. +39 (02) 862-417

POLAND

Augustow — ul Arnikowa 5, 16-300 Augustow/ Tel. & fax +48 (119) 46147
Bedzin — ul. Promyka 31, 42-500 Bedzin
Gdansk — ul. Cedrowa 5, Gdansk 80-125 (mail: MTSK 80-958 Gdansk 50 skr. poczt. 364)/ Tel. +48 (58) 329665
Krakow — ul. Podedworze 23a, 30-686 Krakow/ Tel. +48 (12) 588283
Lublin — ul Bursztynowa 12/52 (mail: Hare Kryszna, 20-001 Lublin 1, P.O. Box 196)/ Tel. +48 (81) 560685
Walbrzych — ul Schmidta 1/5, 58-300 Walbrzych/ Tel. +48 (74) 23185
Warsaw — Mysiadlo k. Warszawy, ul. Zakret 11, 05-500 Piaseczno (mail: MTSK 02-770 Warszawa 130, P.O. Box 257) / Tel. & fax +48 (22) 756-27-11
Wroclaw — ul. Bierutowska 23, 51-317 Wroclaw (mail: MTSK 50-900 Wroclaw, P.O. Box 858)/ Tel. & fax +48 (71) 250-981

FARM COMMUNITY

New Santipura — Czarnow 21, k. Kamiennej gory, woj. Jelenia gora/ Tel. +48 8745-1892

SWEDEN

Gothenburg — Hojdgatan 22, 431 36 Moelndal/ Tel. +46 (031) 879648
Grödinge — Korsnäs Gård, 14792 Grödinge/ Tel. +46 (8530) 29151

Karlstad — Vastra torgg. 16, 65224 Karlstad
Lund — Bredgatan 28 ipg, 222 21/ Tel. +46 (046) 120413
Malmö — Föreningsgatan 28, 21152 Malmö/ Tel. +46 (040) 6116497; restaurant: 6116496
Stockholm — Fridhemsgatan 22, 11240 Stockholm/ Tel. +46 (08) 6549 002
Uppsala — Nannaskolan sal F 3, Kungsgatan 22 (mail: Box 833, 751 08, Uppsala)/ Tel. +46 (018) 102924 or 509956

FARM COMMUNITY

Järna — Almviks Gård, 153 95 Järna/ Tel. +46 (8551) 52050; 52105

ADDITIONAL RESTAURANTS

Göthenburg — Govinda's, Storgatan 20,S-411 38 Göthenburg / Tel. +46 (031) 139698
Malmö — Higher Taste, Amiralsgatan 6, S-211 55 Malmö/ Tel. +46 (040) 970600
Umea — Govinda's, Pilg. 28, 90331 Umea/ Tel. +46 (090) 178875

SWITZERLAND

Basel — Hammerstrasse 11, 4058 Basel/ Tel. +41 (061) 693 26 38
Bern — Marktgasse 7, 3011 Bern/ Tel. +41 (031) 312 38 25
Lugano — Via ai Grotti, 6862 Rancate (TI)/ Tel. +41 (091) 646 66 16
Zürich — Bergstrasse 54, 8030 Zürich/ Tel. +41 (1) 262-33-88
Zürich — Preyergrasse 16, 8001 Zürich/ Tel. +41 (1) 251-88-59

OTHER COUNTRIES

Amsterdam, The Netherlands — Van Hilligaertstraat 17, 1072 JX, Amsterdam/ Tel. +31 (020) 6751404
Antwerp, Belgium — Amerikalei 184, 2000 Antwerpen/ Tel. +32 (03) 237-0037
Barcelona, Spain — c/de L'Oblit 67, 08026 Barcelona/ Tel. +34 (93) 347-9933
Belgrade, Serbia — VVZ-Veda, Custendilska 17, 11000 Beograd/ Tel. +381 (11) 781-695
Budapest, Hungary — Hare Krishna Temple, Mariaremetei ut. 77, Budapest 1028 II/Tel. +36 (01) 1768774
Copenhagen, Denmark — Baunevej 23, 3400 Hillerød/ Tel. +45 42286446
Debrecen, Hungary — L. Hegyi Mihalyne, U62, Debrecen 4030/ Tel. +36 (052) 342-496
Helsinki, Finland — Ruoholahdenkatu 24 D (III krs) 00180, Helsinki/ Tel. +358 (0) 6949879
Iasi, Romania — Stradela Moara De Vint 72, 6600 Iasi
Kaunas, Lithuania — Savanoryu 37, Kaunas/ Tel. +370 (07) 222574
Ljubljana, Slovenia — Zibertova 27, 61000 Ljubljana/ Tel. +386 (061) 131-23-19
Madrid, Spain — Espíritu Santo 19, 28004 Madrid/ Tel. +34 (91) 521-3096
Málaga, Spain — Ctra. Alora, 3 int., 29140 Churriana/ Tel. +34 (952) 621038
Oslo, Norway — Jonsrudvej 1G, 0274 Oslo/ Tel. +47 (022) 552243
Paris, France — 31 Rue Jean Vacquier, 93160 Noisy le Grand/ Tel. +33 (01) 43043263
Plovdiv, Bulgaria — ul. Prosveta 56, Kv. Proslav, Plovdiv 4015/ Tel. +359 (032) 446962
Porto, Portugal — Rua S. Miguel, 19 C.P. 4000 (mail: Apartado 4108, 4002 Porto Codex)/ Tel. +351 (02) 2005469
Prague, Czech Republic — Jilova 290, Prague 5-Zlicin 155 00/ Tel. +42 (02) 3021282 or 3021608
Pula, Croatia — Vinkuran centar 58, 52000 Pula (mail: P.O. Box 16)/ Tel. & fax +385 (052) 573581
Rijeka, Croatia — Svetog Jurja 32, 51000 Rijeka (mail: P.O. Box 61)/ Tel. & fax +385 (051) 263404
Riga, Latvia — 56 Krishyana Barona, LV 1011/ Tel. +371 (02) 272490
Rotterdam, The Netherlands — Braamberg 45, 2905 BK Capelle a/d Yssel./ Tel. +31 (010) 4580873
Santa Cruz de Tenerife, Spain — C/ Castillo, 44, 4°, Santa Cruz 38003,Tenerife/ Tel. +34 (922) 241035
Sarajevo, Bosnia-Herzegovina — Saburina 11, 71000 Sarajevo/ Tel. +381 (071) 531-154
Septon-Durbuy, Belgium — Chateau de Petite Somme, 6940 Septon-Durbuy/ Tel. +32 (086) 322926
Skopje, Macedonia — Vvz. "ISKCON," Roze Luksemburg 13, 91000 Skopje/ Tel. +389 (091) 201451
Sofia, Bulgaria — Villa 3, Vilna Zona-Iztok, Simeonovo, Sofia 1434/ Tel. +359 (02) 6352608
Split, Croatia — Cesta Mutogras 26, 21312 Podstrana, Split (mail: P.O. Box 290, 21001 Split)/ Tel. +385 (021) 651137
Tallinn, Estonia — ul Linnamae Tee 11-97/ Tel. +372 (0142) 59756
Timisoara, Romania — ISKCON, Porumbescu 92, 1900 Timisoara/ Tel. +40 (961) 54776
Vienna, Austria — ISKCON, Rosenackerstrasse 26, 1170 Vienna/ Tel. +43 (01) 455830
Vilnius, Lithuania — Raugyklos G. 23-1, 2024 Vilnius/ Tel. +370 (0122) 66-12-18
Zagreb, Croatia — Bizek 5,10000 Zagreb (mail: P.O. Box 68, 10001 Zagreb)/ Tel. & fax +385 (01) 190548

FARM COMMUNITIES

Czech Republic — Krsnuv Dvur c. 1, 257 28 Chotysany
France (Bhaktivedanta Village) — Chateau Bellevue, F-39700 Chatenois/ Tel. +33 (084) 728235
France (La Nouvelle Mayapura) — Domaine d'Oublaisse, 36360, Lucay le Mâle/ Tel. +33 (054) 402481
Spain (New Vraja Mandala) — (Santa Clara) Brihuega, Guadalajara/ Tel. +34 (911) 280018

ADDITIONAL RESTAURANTS

Barcelona, Spain — Restaurante Govinda, Plaza de la Villa de Madrid 4-5, 08002 Barcelona
Copenhagen, Denmark — Govinda's, Noerre Farimagsgade 82/ Tel. +45 33337444
Oslo, Norway — Krishna's Cuisine, Kirkeveien 59B, 0364 Oslo/ Tel. +47 22606250
Prague, Czech Republic — Govinda's, Soukenicka 27, 110 00 Prague-1/ Tel. +42 (02) 2481-6631, 2481-6016
Prague, Czech Republic — Govinda's, Na hrazi 5, 180 00 Prague 8-Liben/ Tel. +42 (02) 683-7226
Vienna, Austria — Govinda, Lindengasse 2A, 1070 Vienna/ Tel. +43 (01) 5222817

C. I. S. (Commonwealth of Independent States)

RUSSIA

Moscow — Khoroshevskoye shosse d.8, korp.3, 125 284, Moscow/ Tel. +7 (095) 255-67-11

Moscow — Nekrasovsky pos., Dmitrovsky reg., 141760 Moscow/ Tel. +7 (095) 979-8268
Nijni Novgorod — ul. Ivana Mochalova, 7-69, 603904 Nijni Novgorod/ Tel. +7 (8312) 252592
Novosibirsk — ul. Leningradskaya 111-20, Novosibirsk
Perm (Ural Region) — Pr. Mira, 113-142, 614065 Perm/ Tel. +7 (3442) 335740
St. Petersburg — 17, Bumazhnaya st., 198020 St. Petersburg/ Tel. +7 (0812) 186-7259
Ulyanovsk — ul Glinki, 10 /Tel. +7 (0842) 221-42-89
Vladivostok — ul. Ridneva 5-1, 690087 Vladivostok/ Tel. +7 (4232) 268943

UKRAINE

Dnepropetrovsk — ul. Ispolkomovskaya, 56A, 320029 Dnepropetrovsk/ Tel. +380 (0562) 445029
Donetsk — ul. Tubensa, 22, 339018 Makeyevka/ Tel. +380 (0622) 949104
Kharkov — ul. Verhnyogievskaya, 43, 310015 Kharkov/ Tel. +380 (0572) 202167 or 726968
Kiev — ul. Menjinskogo, 21-B., 252054 Kiev/Tel. +380 (044) 2444944
Nikolayev — Sudostroitelny pereulok, 5/8, Nikolayev 327052/ Tel. +380 (0512) 351734
Simferopol — ul. Kievskaya 149/15, 333000 Simferopol/ Tel. +380 (0652) 225116
Vinnitza — ul. Chkalov St., 5, Vinnitza 26800/ Tel. +380 (0432) 323152

OTHER COUNTRIES

Alma Ata, Kazakstan — Per Kommunarov, 5, 480022 Alma Ata/ Tel. +7 (3272) 353830
Baku, Azerbaijan — Pos. 8-i km, per. Sardobi 2, Baku 370060/ Tel. +7 (8922) 212376
Bishkek, Kyrgizstan — Per. Omski, 5, 720000 Bishkek/ Tel. +7 (3312) 472683
Dushanbe, Tadjikistan — ul Anzob, 38, 724001 Dushanbe/ Tel. +7 (3772) 271830
Kishinev, Moldova — ul. Popovich 13, Kishinev/ Tel. +7 (0422) 558099
Minsk, Belarus — ul. Pavlova 11, 220 053 Minsk/ Tel. +7 (0172) 37-4751
Sukhumi, Georgia — Pr. Mira 274, Sukhumi
Tbilisi, Georgia — ul. Kacharava, 16, 380044 Tbilisi/ Tel. +7 (8832) 623326
Yerevan, Armenia — ul. Krupskoy 18, 375019 Yerevan/ Tel. +7 (8852) 275106

AUSTRALASIA

AUSTRALIA

Canberra — 15 Parkhill St., Pearce ACT 2607 (mail: GPO Box 1411, Canberra 2601)/ Tel. +61 (06) 290-1869
Melbourne — 197 Danks St., Albert Park, Victoria 3206 (mail: P.O. Box 125)/ Tel. +61 (03) 969 95122
Perth — 356 Murray St., Perth (mail: P.O. Box 102, Bayswater, W. A. 6053)/ Tel. +61 (09) 481-1114 or 370-1552 (evenings)
Sydney — 180 Falcon St., North Sydney, N.S.W. 2060 (mail: P. O. Box 459, Cammeray, N.S.W.2062)/ Tel. +61 (02) 9959-4558
Sydney — 3296 King St., Newtown 2042/ Tel. +61 (02) 550-6524

FARM COMMUNITIES

Bambra (New Nandagram) — Oak Hill, Dean's Marsh Rd., Bambra, VIC 3241/ Tel. +61 (052) 88-7383
Millfield, N.S.W. — New Gokula Farm, Lewis Lane (off Mt.View Rd. Millfield near Cessnock), N.S.W. (mail: P.O. Box 399, Cessnock 2325, N.S.W.)/ Tel. +61 (049) 98-1800
Murwillumbah (New Govardhana) — Tyalgum Rd., Eungella, via Murwillumbah N. S. W. 2484 (mail: P.O. Box 687)/ Tel. +61 (066) 72-6579

ADDITIONAL RESTAURANTS

Adelaide — Food for Life, 79 Hindley St./ Tel. +61 (08) 2315258
Brisbane — Govinda's, 1st •oor, 99 Elizabeth Street/ Tel. +61 (07) 210-0255
Brisbane — Hare Krishna Food for Life, 190 Brunswick St. Fortitude Valley/ Tel. +61 (070) 854-1016
Melbourne — Crossways, Floor 1, 123 Swanston St., Melbourne, Victoria 3000/ Tel. +61 (03) 9650-2939
Melbourne — Gopal's, 139 Swanston St., Melbourne, Victoria 3000/ Tel. +61 (03) 9650-1578
Perth — Hare Krishna Food for Life, 200 William St., Northbridge, WA 6003/ Tel. +61 (09) 227-1684

NEW ZEALAND, FIJI, AND PAPUA NEW GUINEA

Christchurch, New Zealand — 83 Bealey Ave. (mail: P.O. Box 25-190 Christchurch)/ Tel. +64 (03) 3665-174
Labasa, Fiji — Delailabasa (mail: P.O. Box 133)/ Tel. +679 812912
Lautoka, Fiji — 5 Tavewa Ave. (mail: P.O. Box 125)/ Tel. +679 664112
Port Moresby, Papua New Guinea — Section 23, Lot 46, Gordonia St., Hohola (mail: P. O. Box 571, POM NCD)/ Tel. +675 259213
Rakiraki, Fiji — Rewasa, Rakiraki (mail: P.O. Box 204)/ Tel. +679 694243
Suva, Fiji — Nasinu 7½ miles (mail: P.O. Box 7315)/ Tel. +679 393599
Wellington, New Zealand — 60 Wade St., Wadestown, Wellington (mail: P.O. Box 2753, Wellington)/ Tel. +64 (04) 4720510

FARM COMMUNITY

Auckland, New Zealand (New Varshan) — Hwy. 18, Riverhead, next to Huapai Golf Course (mail: R.D. 2, Kumeu, Auckland)/ Tel. +64 (09) 4128075

RESTAURANTS

Auckland, New Zealand — Gopal's, Civic House (1st •oor), 291 Queen St./ Tel. +64 (09) 3034885
Christchurch, New Zealand — Gopal's, 143 Worcester St./ Tel. +64 (03) 3667-035
Labasa, Fiji — Hare Krishna Restaurant, Naseakula Road/ Tel. +679 811364
Lautoka, Fiji — Gopal's, Corner of Yasawa St. and Naviti St./ Tel. +679 662990
Suva, Fiji — Gopal's, 18 Pratt St./ Tel. +679 314154

AFRICA

NIGERIA

Abeokuta — Ibadan Rd., Obanatoka (mail: P.O. Box 5177)

Benin City — 108 Lagos Rd., Uselu/ Tel. +234 (052) 247900
Enugu — 8 Church Close, off College Rd., Housing Estate, Abakpa-Nike
Ibadan — 1 Ayo Akintoba St., Agbowo, University of Ibadan
Jos — 5A Liberty Dam Close, P.O. Box 6557, Jos
Kaduna — 8B Dabo Rd., Kaduna South, P.O. Box 1121, Kaduna
Lagos — 25 Jaiyeola Ajata St., Ajao Estate, off International Airport Express Rd., Lagos (mail: P.O. Box 8793)/ Tel. & Fax +234 (01) 876169
Port Harcourt — Second Tarred Road, Ogwaja Waterside (mail: P.O. Box 4429, Trans Amadi)
Warri — Okwodiete Village, Kilo 8, Effurun/Orerokpe Rd. (mail: P.O. Box 1922, Warri)

SOUTH AFRICA

Cape Town — 17 St. Andrews Rd., Rondebosch 7700/ Tel. +27 (021) 689-1529
Durban — Chatsworth Centre, Chatsworth 4030 (mail: P.O. Box 56003)/ Tel. +27 (31) 433-328
Johannesburg — 14 Goldreich St., Hillbrow 2001 (mail: P.O. Box 10667, Johannesburg 2000)/ Tel. +27 (011) 484-3273
Port Elizabeth — 18 Strand Fontein Rd., 6001 Port Elizabeth/ Tel. & Fax +27 (41) 53 43 30

OTHER COUNTRIES

Gaborone, Botswana — P.O. Box 201003/ Tel. +267 307 768
Kampala, Uganda — Bombo Rd., near Makerere University (mail: P.O. Box 1647, Kampala)
Kisumu, Kenya — P.O. Box 547/ Tel. +254 (035) 42546
Marondera, Zimbabwe — 6 Pine Street (mail: P.O. Box 339)/ Tel. +263 (028) 8877801
Mombasa, Kenya — Hare Krishna House, Sauti Ya Kenya and Kisumu Rds. (mail: P.O. Box 82224, Mombasa)/ Tel. +254 (011) 312248
Nairobi, Kenya — Muhuroni Close, off West Nagara Rd. (mail: P.O. Box 28946, Nairobi)/ Tel. +254 (02) 744365
Phoenix, Mauritius — Hare Krishna Land, Pont Fer, Phoenix (mail: P. O. Box 108, Quartre Bornes, Mauritius)/ Tel. +230 696-5804
Rose Hill, Mauritius — 13 Gordon St./ Tel. +230 454-5275

FARM COMMUNITY

Mauritius (ISKCON Vedic Farm) — Hare Krishna Rd., Vrindaban, Bon Acceuil/ Tel. +230 418-3955

ASIA

INDIA

Agartala, Tripura — Assam-Agartala Rd., Banamalipur, 799001
Ahmedabad, Gujarat — Sattelite Rd., Gandhinagar Highway Crossing, Ahmedabad 380054/ Tel. (079) 6749827, 6749945
Allahabad, U. P. — 161, Kashi Nagar, Baluaghat, Allahabad 211003/ Tel. 653318
Bamanbore, Gujarat — N.H. 8A, Surendra-nagar District
Bangalore, Karnataka — Hare Krishna Hill, 1 'R' Block, Chord Road, Rajaji Nagar 560010/ Tel. (080) 332 1956
Baroda, Gujarat — Hare Krishna Land, Gotri Rd., 390021/ Tel. (0265) 326299 or 331012
Belgaum, Karnataka — Shukravar Peth, Tilak Wadi, 590006
Bhubaneswar, Orissa — National Highway No. 5, Nayapali, 751001/ Tel. (0674) 413517 or 413475
Bombay — (see Mumbai)
Calcutta, W. Bengal — 3C Albert Rd., 700017/ Tel. (033) 2473757 or 2476075
Chandigarh — Hare Krishna Land, Dakshin Marg, Sector 36-B, 160036/ Tel. (0172) 601590 and 603232
Coimbatore, Tamil Nadu — 387, VGR Puram, Dr. Alagesan Rd., 641011/ Tel. (0422) 445978 or 442749
Gangapur, Gujarat — Bhaktivedanta Rajavidyalaya, Krishnalok, Surat-Bardoli Rd. Gangapur, P.O. Gangadhara, Dist. Surat, 394310/Tel. (02,61) 667075
Gauhati, Assam — Ulubari Charali, Gauhati 781001/ Tel. (0361) 31208
Guntur, A.P. — Opp. Sivalayam, Peda Kakani 522509
Hanumkonda, A.P. — Neeladri Rd., Kapuwada, 506011/ Tel. 08712-77399
Haridwar, U.P. — ISKCON, P.O. Box 4, Haridwar, U.P. 249401/ Tel. (0133) 422655
Hyderabad, A.P. — Hare Krishna Land, Nampally Station Rd., 500001/ Tel. (040) 592018 or 552924
Imphal, Manipur — Hare Krishna Land, Airport Road, 795001/ Tel. (0385) 221587
Jaipur, Rajasthan — P.O. Box 270, Jaipur 302001/ Tel. (0141) 364022
Katra, Jammu, and Kashmir — Srila Prabhupada Ashram, Srila Prabhupada Marg, Kalka Mata Mandir, Katra (Vashnov Mata) 182101/ Tel. (01991) 3047
Kurukshetra, Haryana — 369 Gudri Muhalla, Main Bazaar, 132118/ Tel. (1744) 32806 or 33529
Lucknow, Uttar Pradesh — 1 Ashak Nagar, Guru Govind Singh Marg, 226018
Madras, Tamil Nadu — 59, Burkit Rd., T. Nagar, 600017/ Tel. 443266
Mayapur, W. Bengal — Shree Mayapur Chandrodaya Mandir, Shree Mayapur Dham, Dist. Nadia (mail: P.O. Box 10279, Ballyganj, Calcutta 700019)/ Tel. (03472) 45239 or 45240 or 45233
Moirang, Manipur — Nongban Ingkhon, Tidim Rd./ Tel. 795133
Mumbai, Maharashtra (Bombay) — Hare Krishna Land, Juhu 400 049/ Tel. (022) 6206860
Mumbai, Maharashtra — 7 K. M. Munshi Marg, Chowpatty, 400007/ Tel. (022) 3634078
Mumbai, Maharashtra — Shivaji Chowk, Station Rd., Bhayandar (West), Thane 401101/ Tel. (022) 8191920
Nagpur, Maharashtra — 70 Hill Road, Ramnagar, 440010/ Tel. (0712) 529932
New Delhi — Sant Nagar Main Road (Garhi), behind Nehru Place Complex (mail: P. O. Box 7061), 110065/ Tel. (011) 6419701 or 6412058
New Delhi — 14/63, Punjabi Bagh, 110026/ Tel. (011) 5410782
Pandharpur, Maharashtra — Hare Krsna Ashram (across Chandrabhaga River), Dist. Sholapur, 413304/ Tel. (0218) 623473
Patna, Bihar — Rajendra Nagar Road No. 12, 800016/ Tel. (0612) 50765
Pune, Maharashtra — 4 Tarapoor Rd., Camp, 411001/ Tel. (0212) 667259

Puri, Orissa — Sipasurubuli Puri, Dist. Puri/ (06752) 24592, 24594
Puri, Orissa — Bhakti Kuthi, Swargadwar, Puri/ Tel. (06752) 23740
Secunderabad, A.P. — 27 St. John's Road, 500026/ Tel. (040) 805232
Silchar, Assam — Ambikapatti, Silchar, Cachar Dist., 788004
Siliguri, W. Bengal — Gitalpara, 734401/ Tel. (0353) 26619
Surat, Gujarat — Rander Rd., Jahangirpura, 395005/ Tel. (0261) 685516 or 685891
Sri Rangam, Tamal Nadu — 6A E.V.S. Rd., Sri Rangam, Tiruchirapalli 6/ Tel. 433945
Tirupati, A. P. — K.T. Road, Vinayaka Nagar, 517507/ Tel. (08574) 20114
Trivandrum, Kerala — T.C. 224/1485, WC Hospital Rd., Thycaud, 695014/ Tel. (0471) 68197
Udhampur, Jammu and Kashmir — Srila Prabhupada Ashram, Prabhupada Marg, Prabhupada Nagar, Udhampur 182101/ Tel. (01992) 70298
Vallabh Vidyanagar, Gujarat — ISKCON Hare Krishna Land, 338120/ Tel. (02692) 30796
Vrindavana, U. P. — Krishna-Balaram Mandir, Bhaktivedanta Swami Marg, Raman Reti, Mathura Dist., 281124/ Tel. (0565) 442-478 or 442-355

FARM COMMUNITIES

Ahmedabad District, Gujarat — Hare Krishna Farm, Katwada (contact ISKCON Ahmedabad)
Assam — Karnamadhu, Dist. Karimganj
Chamorshi, Maharashtra — 78 Krishnanagar Dham, Dis. Gadhachiroli, 442603

OTHER COUNTRIES

Cagayan de Oro, Philippines — 30 Dahlia St., Ilaya Carmen, 900 (c/o Sepulveda's Compound)
Chittagong, Bangladesh — Caitanya Cultural Society, Sri Pundarik Dham, Mekhala, Hathzari (mail: GPO Box 877, Chittagong)/ Tel. +88 (031) 225822
Colombo, Sri Lanka — 188 New Chetty St., Colombo 13/ Tel. +94 (01) 433325
Dhaka, Bangladesh — 5 Chandra Mohon Basak St., Banagram, Dhaka 1203/ Tel. +880 (02) 236249
Hong Kong — 27 Chatam Road South, 6/F, Kowloon/ Tel. +852 7396818
Iloilo City, Philippines — 13-1-1 Tereos St., La Paz, Iloilo City, Iloilo/ Tel. +63 (033) 73391
Jakarta, Indonesia — P.O. Box 2694, Jakarta Pusat 10001/ Tel. +62 (021) 4899646
Jessore, Bangladesh — Nitai Gaur Mandir, Kathakhali Bazaar, P. O. Panjia, Dist. Jessore
Jessore, Bangladesh — Rupa-Sanatana Smriti Tirtha, Ramsara, P. O. Magura Hat, Dist. Jessore
Kathmandu, Nepal — Budhanilkantha, Kathmandu (mail: P. O. Box 3520)/ Tel. +977 (01) 290743
Kuala Lumpur, Malaysia — Lot 9901, Jalan Awan Jawa, Taman Yarl, off 5½ Mile, Jalan Kelang Lama, Petaling/ Tel. +60 (03) 780-7355, -7360, or -7369
Manila, Philippines — Penthouse Liwag Bldg., 3307 Mantanzas St., Makati, Metro Manila/ Tel. +63 (02) 8337883 loc. 10
Taipei, Taiwan — (mail: c/o ISKCON Hong Kong)
Tel Aviv, Israel — 16 King George St. (mail: P. O. Box 48163, Tel Aviv 61480)/ Tel. +972 (03) 5285475 or 6299011
Tokyo, Japan — 1-29-2-202 Izumi, Suginami-ku, Tokyo 168/ Tel. +81 (03) 3327-1541
Yogyakarta, Indonesia — P.O. Box 25, Babarsari YK, DIY

FARM COMMUNITIES

Indonesia — Govinda Kunja (contact ISKCON Jakarta)
Malaysia — Jalan Sungai Manik, 36000 Teluk Intan, Perak
Philippines (Hare Krishna Paradise) — 231 Pagsabungan Rd., Basak, Mandaue City/ Tel. +63 (032) 83254

ADDITIONAL RESTAURANTS

Cebu, Philippines — Govinda's, 26 Sanchiangko St.
Kuala Lumpur, Malaysia — Govinda's, 16-1 Jalan Bunus Enam, Masjid India/ Tel. +60 (03) 7807355 or 7807360 or 7807369

LATIN AMERICA

BRAZIL

Belém, PA — Almirante Barroso, Travessa Santa Matilde, 64, Souza/ Tel. +55 (091) 243-0558
Belo Horizonte, MG — Rua Aristoteles Caldeira, 334, Prado/ Tel. +55 (031) 332-8460
Brasilia, DF — CLN 310, Bloco B, Loja 45, Terreo/ Tel. +55 (061) 272-3111
Campos, RJ — Rua Barao de Miracema, 186, Centro
Caruaru, PE — Rua Major Sinval, 180, 1º Andar
Curitiba, PR — Al. Cabral, 670, Centro/ Tel. +55 (041) 277-3176
Florianopolis, SC — Rua Laurindo Januario Silveira, 3250, Canto da Lagoa
Fortaleza, CE — Rua Jose Lourenço, 2114, Aldeota/ Tel. +55 (085) 264-1273
Goiania, GO — Rua 24A, 20 (esq. Av. Parananba)/ Tel. +55 (062) 224-9820
Guarulhos, SP — Rua Orixas, 1, Jardim Afonso/ Tel. +55 (011) 209-6669
Manaus, AM — Av. 7 de Setembro, 1599, Centro/ Tel. +55 (092) 232-0202
Petropolis, RJ — Rua do Imperador, 349, Sobrado
Porto Alegre, RS — Av. Basian, 396, Menino Deus/ Tel. +55 (051) 233-1474
Recife, PE — Rua Democlitos de Souza Filho, 235, Madalena
Ribeirao Preto, SP — Rua dos Aliados, 155, Campos Eliseos/ Tel. +55 (016) 628-1533
Rio de Janeiro, RJ — Rua Barao da Torre, 199, apt. 102, Ipanema/ Tel. +55 (021) 267-0052
Salvador, BA — Rua Alvaro Adorno, 17, Brotas/ Tel. +55 (071) 382-1064
Santos, SP — Rua Nabuco de Araujo, 151, Embare/ Tel. +55 (0132) 38-4655
São Carlos, SP — Rua Emilio Ribas, 195
São Paulo, SP — Av. Angelica, 2583/Tel. +55 (011) 259-7352
São Paulo, SP — Rua Otavio Tarquino de Souza, 299, Congonhas/ Tel. +55 (011) 536-4010

FARM COMMUNITIES

Autazes, AM — Nova Jarikandha/ Tel. +55 (092) 232-0202
Caruaru, PE — Nova Vrajadhama, Distrito de Murici, CP 283, CEP 55000-000
Curitiba, PR — Nova Goloka, Planta Carla, Pinhais

Parati, RJ — Goura Vrindavan, Bairro de Grauna, CP 062, CEP 23970-000
Pindamonhangaba, SP — Nova Gokula, Bairro Ribeiro Grande, CP 108, CEP 12400-000/ Tel. +55 (012) 982-9036
Teresopolis, RJ — Vrajabhumi, Canoas, CP 92687, CEP 25951-970

MEXICO

Guadalajara — Pedro Moreno No. 1791, Sector Juarez/ Tel. +52 (38) 160775
Mexico City — Gob. Tiburcio Montiel No. 45, 11850 Mexico, D.F./ Tel. +52 (5) 271-22-23
Saltillo — Blvd. Saltillo No. 520, Col. Buenos Aires

FARM COMMUNITY

Guadalajara — Contact ISKCON Guadalajara

ADDITIONAL RESTAURANTS

Orizaba — Restaurante Radhe, Sur 5 No. 50, Orizaba, Ver./ Tel. +52 (272) 5-75-25

PERU

Lima — Pasaje Solea 101 Santa Maria-Chosica/ Tel. +51 (014) 910891
Lima — Schell 634 Mira•ores
Lima — Av. Garcilazo de la Vega 1670-1680/ Tel. +51 (014) 259523

FARM COMMUNITY

Correo De Bella Vista — DPTO De San Martin

ADDITIONAL RESTAURANT

Cuzco — Espaderos 128

OTHER COUNTRIES

Asunción, Paraguay — Centro Bhaktivedanta, Mariano R. Alonso 925, Asunción/ Tel. +595 (021) 480-266
Bogotá, Colombia — Calle 72, nro.20-60, Bogota (mail: Apartado Aereo 58680, Zona 2, Chapinero)/ Tel. & Fax +57 (01) 2554529, 2482234
Buenos Aires, Argentina — Centro Bhaktivedanta, Andonaegui 2054 (1431)/ Tel. +54 (01) 521- 5567, 523-4232
Cali, Colombia — Avenida 2 EN, #24N-39/ Tel. +57 (023) 68-88-53
Caracas, Venezuela — Avenida Berlin, Quinta Tia Lola, La California Norte/ Tel. +58 (02) 225463
Chinandega, Nicaragua — Edificio Hare Krsna No. 108, Del Banco Nacional 10 mts. abajo/ Tel. +505 (341) 2359
Cochabamba, Bolivia — Av. Heroinas E-0435 Apt. 3 (mail: P. O. Box 2070)/ Tel. & Fax +591 (042) 54346
Essequibo Coast, Guyana — New Navadvipa Dham, Mainstay, Essequibo Coast
Georgetown, Guyana — 24 Uitvlugt Front, West Coast Demerara
Guatemala, Guatemala — Apartado Postal 1534
Guayaquil, Ecuador — 6 de Marzo 226 or V. M. Rendon/ Tel. +593 (04) 308412 y 309420
Managua, Nicaragua — Residencial Bolonia, De Galeria los Pipitos 75 mts. norte (mail: P.O. Box 772)/ Tel. +505 242759
Mar del Plata, Argentina — Dorrego 4019 (7600) Mar del Plata/ Tel. +54 (023) 745688
Montevideo, Uruguay — Centro de Bhakti-Yoga, Mariano Moreno 2660, Montevideo/ Tel. +598 (02) 477919
Panama, Republic of Panama — Via las Cumbres, entrada Villa Zaita, frente a INPSA No.1 (mail: P.O. Box 6-29-54, Panama)
Pereira, Colombia — Carrera 5a, #19-36
Quito, Ecuador — Inglaterra y Amazonas
Rosario, Argentina — Centro de Bhakti-Yoga, Paraguay 556, (2000) Rosario/ Tel. +54 (041) 252630, 264243
San José, Costa Rica — Centro Cultural Govinda, Av. 7, Calles 1 y 3, 235 mtrs. norte del Banco Anglo, San Pedro (mail: Apdo. 166,1002)/ Tel. +5206 23-52 38
San Salvador, El Salvador — Avenida Universitaria 1132, Media Quadra al sur de la Embajada Americana (mail: P.O. Box 1506)/ Tel. +503 25-96-17
Santiago, Chile — Carrera 330/ Tel. +56 (02) 698-8044
Santo Domingo, Dominican Republic — Calle Cayetano Rodriquez No. 254/ Tel. (809) 686-5665
Trinidad and Tobago, West Indies — Orion Drive, Debe/ Tel. +1 (809) 647-3165
Trinidad and Tobago, West Indies — Prabhupada Ave. Longdenville, Chaguanas

FARM COMMUNITIES

Argentina (Bhaktilata Puri) — Casilla de Correo No 77, 1727 Marcos Paz, Pcia. Bs. As., Republica Argentina
Bolivia — Contact ISKCON Cochabamba
Colombia (Nueva Mathura) — Cruzero del Guali, Municipio de Caloto, Valle del Cauca/ Tel. 612688 en Cali
Costa Rica — Nueva Goloka Vrindavana, Carretera a Paraiso, de la entrada del Jardin Lancaster (por Calle Concava), 200 metros al sur (mano derecha) Cartago (mail: Apdo. 166, 1002)/ Tel. +506 551-6752
Ecuador (Nueva Mayapur) — Ayampe (near Guayaquil)
Ecuador (Giridharidesha) — Chordeleg (near Cuenca), Cassiga Postal 01.05.1811, Cuenca/ Tel. +593 (7) 255735
El Salvador — Carretera a Santa Ana, Km. 34, Canton Los Indios, Zapotitan, Dpto. de La Libertad
Guyana — Seawell Village, Corentyne, East Berbice

ADDITIONAL RESTAURANTS

Buenos Aires, Argentina — Gusto Superior, Blanco Encalada 2722, 1428 Buenos Aires Cap. Fed./ Tel. +54 (01) 788 3023
Cochabamba, Bolivia — Gopal Restaurant, calle España N-0250 (Galeria Olimpia) (mail: P. O. Box 2070, Cochabamba)/ Tel. +591 (042) 26626
Guatemala, Guatemala — Callejor Santandes a una cuadra abajo de Guatel, Panajachel Solola
San Salvador, El Salvador — 25 Avenida Norte 1132
Santa Cruz, Bolivia — Snack Govinda, Av. Argomosa (1ero anillo), esq. Bolivar/ Tel. +591 (03) 345189

Stay in touch with Krishna

Read more from *Back to Godhead* magazine—
6 months for only $9.95! (Offer valid in US only.)

SPECIAL TRIAL OFFER!

YES, please send me *Back to Godhead* magazine.

❒ Enter my subscription for 6 months (3 issues) for only $9.95 (US only, please)

❒ Enter my subscription for 1 year (6 issues) for only $17.95 (save 25% off the cover price). For Canada, add $3. All other countries, add $9. (Payment must be in US funds drawn on a US bank.)

❒ Bill me ❒ Payment enclosed ❒ Credit card

Name ______________________________

Address ______________________ Tel. ____________

City ________________ ST ______ Zip ____________

Card no. ____________________ Exp. date __________

Signature ______________________________

Mail or fax this coupon to:

BTG Service Center, P.O. Box 255, Sandy Ridge, NC 27046, USA

For faster service, call toll free: 1-800-800-3284

BHAGAVAD-GĪTĀ AS IT IS

The world's most popular edition of a timeless classic.

Throughout the ages, the world's greatest minds have turned to the *Bhagavad-gītā* for answers to life's perennial questions. Renowned as the jewel of India's spiritual wisdom, the *Gītā* summarizes the profound Vedic knowledge concerning man's essential nature, his environment, and ultimately his relationship with God. With more than fifty million copies sold in twenty languages, *Bhagavad-gītā As It Is,* by His Divine Grace A.C. Bhaktivedanta Swami Prabhupāda, is the most widely read edition of the *Gītā* in the world. It includes the original Sanskrit text, phonetic transliterations, word-for-word meanings, translation, elaborate commentary, and many full-color illustrations. (Pocket version: translation and commentary only.)

Pocket	Vinyl	Hard	Deluxe
$4.50	$8.50	$9.95	$19.95
BGS	BGV	BGH	BGD

ORDER TOLL FREE 1-800-927-4152

GREAT
VEGETARIAN DISHES

Featuring over 100 stunning full-color photos, this book is for spiritually aware people who want the exquisite taste of Hare Krishna cooking without a lot of time in the kitchen. The 240 international recipes were tested and refined by the author, world-famous Hare Krishna chef Kūrma dāsa.

240 recipes, 192 pages, coffee-table-size hardback

US: $19.95 #GVD

THE HARE KRISHNA BOOK OF
VEGETARIAN COOKING

This colorfully illustrated, practical cookbook by Ādirāja dāsa not only helps you prepare authentic Indian dishes at home but also teaches you about the ancient tradition behind India's world-famous vegetarian cuisine.

130 kitchen-tested recipes, 300 pages, hardback

US: $11.50 #HKVC

BEYOND BIRTH AND DEATH

What's the self? Can it exist apart from the physical body? If so, what happens to the self at the time of death? What about reincarnation? Liberation? In *Beyond Birth and Death* Śrīla Prabhupāda answers these intriguing questions and more.

Softbound, 96 pages

US$1.00 #BBD

THE HIGHER TASTE

A Guide to Gourmet Vegetarian Cooking and a Karma-Free Diet

Illustrated profusely with black-and-white drawings and eight full-color plates, this popular volume contains over 60 tried and tested international recipes, together with the why's and how's of the Krishna conscious vegetarian life-style.

Softbound, 176 pages

US$1.50 #HT

LIFE COMES FROM LIFE

In this historic series of talks with his disciples, Śrīla Prabhupāda uncovers the hidden and blatantly unfounded assumptions that underlie currently fashionable doctrines concerning the origins and purpose of life.

Softbound, 96 pages

US$1.50 #LCFL

CIVILIZATION AND TRANSCENDENCE

In this book Śrīla Prabhupāda calls the bluff of modern materialistic culture: "Modern so-called civilization is simply a dog's race. The dog is running on four legs, and modern people are running on four wheels. The learned, astute person will use this life to gain what he has missed in countless prior lives—namely, realization of self and realization of God."

Softbound, 90 pages

US$1.00 #CT

Posters

Superb Florentino linen embossed prints. All posters are 18 x 24. (Besides the three shown, there are ten others to choose from. Call for our *free* catalog.)

US$3.75 each #POS

Śrī Viṣṇu

Mantra Meditation Kit

Includes a string of 108 hand-carved *japa* beads, a cotton carrying bag, counter beads, and instructions.

US$5.00 #MMK

Pārtha Sārathi

The Rādhā-Kṛṣṇa Temple Album

The original Apple LP produced by George Harrison, featuring the Hare Kṛṣṇa Mantra and the "Govindam" prayers that are played daily in ISKCON temples around the world. On stereo cassette or CD.

US$3.75 for cassette #CC-6
US$11.25 for CD #CD-6

Śrīla Prabhupāda

Śrīla Prabhupāda Chanting Japa

This recording of His Divine Grace A.C. Bhaktivedanta Swami Prabhupāda chanting *japa* is a favorite among young and old devotees alike.

US$2.95 for cassette #JT-1

Incense

Twenty sticks per pack, hand rolled in India. Highest quality, packed in foil.

US$1.50 per pack #INC

ORDER TOLL FREE 1-800-927-4152

Order Form

Make check or money order payable to The Bhaktivedanta Book Trust and send to:

The Bhaktivedanta Book Trust
Dept. DHA-H
3764 Watseka Avenue • Los Angeles, CA 90034

Name ______________________________
Please Print

Address ______________________________

City ____________________ ST ______ Zip __________

Code	Description	Qty.	Price	Total

Subtotal US $ __________

CA Sales Tax 8.25% US $ __________

Shipping 15% of Subtotal (minimum $2.00) US $ __________

TOTAL US $ __________

To Place a Credit Card Order Please Call

1-800-927-4152

VISA MasterCard

For a free catalog call:

1-800-927-4152